WHAT THE LONE WOLF DREAMS

WHAT THE LONE WOLF DREAMS

Selected Works From the COMPAS
Writers & Artists in the Schools Program

Edited by
Kelly Barnhill

Illustrations by
Rogger Cummings

COMPAS
Writers & Artists in the Schools
2008

Publication of this book is generously supported by the Lillian Wright and C. Emil Berglund Foundation, dedicated in memory of C. Emil Berglund.

COMPAS programs are made possible in part by grants provided by the Minnesota State Arts Board, through an appropriation by the Minnesota State Legislature. Additional support has been provided by many generous corporations and foundations which can be found at our website www.compas.org/pages/artsedfunders.html.

As always, we are grateful for the hundreds of excellent teachers throughout Minnesota who sponsor COMPAS Writers & Artists in the Schools residencies. Without their support and hard work, the writers and artists would not weave their magic, and the student work we celebrate in this book would not spring to life.

Book Production: Betsy Mowry, Arts Education Associate; and
                 Daniel Gabriel, Arts Education Programs Director.
Book Design: Betsy Mowry

ISBN 0-927663-43-0

Illustrations ©2008 by Rogger Cummings
Music, Additional Words, Arrangements ©2008 by Charlie Maguire
and Mello-Jamin Music
Text ©2008 COMPAS

COMPAS
Suite 304
75 Fifth Street West
St. Paul, Minnesota 55102-1496

Bob Olsen, Executive Director
Daniel Gabriel, Arts Education Programs Director

COMPAS strengthens people and communities in Minnesota by engaging them in making art.

What the Lone Wolf Dreams is dedicated to Ron Clark,
long-time Editorial Page Editor at the *Saint Paul Pioneer Press*, who,
as a Board member of COMPAS and a community leader,
tirelessly committed himself to furthering opportunities
for creative self-expression.

WHAT THE LONE WOLF DREAMS
Table of Contents

Singing To The Stars

I Had The Sun In My Lap

WHAT THE LONE WOLF DREAMS

Introduction

I was seated comfortably on a city bus, writing commentary on my students' stories when a woman sat down and peered over my shoulder.

"You're a teacher," she said without a question mark.

"Indeed I am," I said, as I scribbled a smiley face in the margin of a particularly awesome paragraph.

"I can't stand teachers," she said. I clicked my pen closed and slipped it into my bag. Before I could ask her why, she continued:

"They've always struck me as the type who just can't move on and grow up. At some point, you have to be an adult." She gazed pointedly at the smiley face and pursed her lips.

I said nothing. Honestly, what was there to say? Because what she said was perfectly true: I teach writing to students as a way of forcing myself away from the lure of adulthood. Moreover, it is the periodic return to the dynamism and passion of youth that invigorates my own writing process. I'll tell you a secret: When I teach a creative writing residency in a school, I get so much more from my students than I could ever give. Don't tell anyone, or I'll never make a living doing this.

Given that this is my first time editing the COMPAS anthology, I read, re-read and re-re-read each piece, trying to weave together these divergent, tremulous voices into a unified, harmonic whole. While the unification was a time consuming and delightful process—and necessary in order to pull together the volume you have here—it was the individual voices that I found so arresting, and brave.

In the first section, "I am a Diamond in the Dirt," students respond to the world around them—family, community and nature. Edith Hernandez's heartbreaking poem, "For My Brother" and Ciera Hardyman's poem "Rage" both show families in turmoil, one due to the death of a family member, and one due to a complicated parental relationship. Damien D. Mobley Jr.'s untitled poem (the first line from which the title of this section is derived), depicts a young man who implicitly knows his own value, even if the rest of the world is slower to recognize it, while Mustafa Shabazz's piece, "So You Wanna Be Bad?" is a voice of caution to another person who is all too willing to sell himself short. Pay special attention to Jack Lutz's haunting and quietly joyful "I Love Nothing," as well as to Debbie Le's untitled piece about a bad girl gone good.

The second section, "Minnesota Blues," is the musical interlude of the anthology. This year, many classrooms participated in a songwriting workshop, learning the painstaking process of collaboration. These songs reflect the classes as cultural entities, and, as observers, we can see what is important to these young artists.

The third section, "Singing to the Stars," is a group of short stories and essays. In each of these pieces are main characters struggling to identify and define their talents and futures in the context of a confusing and chaotic world. "Making Choices" tells the story of a girl trying to do the right thing while being pressured by bullies, while "Singing to the Stars" brings us the story of a young boy who discovers his own special talent.

In the last section, "I Had the Sun in my Lap," the fantastic and the mundane interact in poetic and surprising ways. Here our writers experiment with surrealism, magical realism, folk tale, fantasy—all existing in that nebulous space between the known and the unknown. "Three Magical Foxes," in the classic fairy tale tradition, is an imaginative and inventive tale of three foxes on a fantastical adventure. "I Was Reading a Poem," describes the mystical collaboration between reading and thinking. "The Day Cambree's Artwork Came to Life," tells just that—what happens to the artist when her art suddenly has a mind of its own? That's a question I don't much like to think about—I don't know what I'd do if one of my own villains suddenly showed up for tea. However, the more I thought about it, the more compelling I found the idea, and that day in my writing session, my villain showed up bearing tea bags and cream. It was, in the end, a delightful conversation.

Which brings me back to my original point. Were it not for my connection to the flexibility and vigor of youth, I would not be the writer I am today. For every student who writes a story in my class, there are ten stories making their way through my head, hands and papers. Does this mean I'm not really an adult? Am I simply refusing to "move on" by hanging out with a bunch of school kids and writing stories? Well, yes and no. And that's the point, isn't it?

An artist residency is an exercise in *both*. Let me explain: during our time in the classroom, we are *both* student and teacher, *both* creative and analytical, *both* working and playing, *both* growing and grown. It is the ability to be both that allows for a multi-dimensional perspective on the world around us, a widening of eye and ear and mind. It is the gift of *both* that my students give me every time I walk into a classroom. If I can reciprocate, if my students similarly can be *both*, even if it's only for a week, then I'm doing my job.

Kelly Barnhill

WHAT THE LONE WOLF DREAMS

A Note to Teachers

Dear Teachers,

First off, on behalf of my fellow Artists, I want to express my deepest thanks for opening your classrooms to us and allowing us to share our passion for our various disciplines with your students. None of us would be doing this work if we didn't utterly love it. And we do. Spending a week making art with a classroom full of completely awesome kids is something that every artist should experience at least once in their lives. And every kid should have the opportunity to work intensively with a professional artist, even if it's only for a little while. Given the state of arts funding in the schools these days, it's tougher and tougher to push arts education in schools whose budgets are not balanced. That you advocated for this program speaks to your commitment to a broad education for your beloved students. And on their behalf as well, I thank you again.

That being said, I have some specific ideas on the use and methodology for this volume of student work in your classroom. Or, to be more clear, a singular, specific idea, and it is this: Do not teach this book.

Allow me to clarify. It is not—not for a moment—that I do not trust the soundness of your methods or the dynamic and inventive ways in which you operate your classrooms. Of course you do. You're *that* kind of teacher. However, there are some things that must be discovered, and *discovery*, by its nature, is a product of serendipity, happenstance and luck.

The purpose of this book is to highlight and celebrate the wonderful work of our student writers. But it has another purpose as well. A *secret* purpose. This book is also meant to whisper in the shadows, to creep into the curling fingers of the exact child who needs it. There are students in your classroom who are closet writers. They scribble lines into the bottoms of their desks or invent stories in their heads when they should be reading an essay on the New Deal. These students will not write if you ask them to, nor will they connect with the stories taught in class. They must discover on their own. This book, at its heart, is for them. It is to remind them that they are not alone, that one day, their voice will be heard.

This book must be hidden in plain sight. This book must be stumbled upon. This book must be surreptitiously strewn in randomized (yet deviously clever) locations. Here are a few ideas:

- Casually leave a copy on top of the empty paper towels dispenser in the boy's bathroom.
- While in the lunchroom, slide it onto the dessert table (somewhere between the butterscotch pudding and the fluorescent green jell-o).
- Drop a copy or two in the Detention room. Or in the waiting area of the Vice Principal's office.
- Hide a copy in the Varsity locker room. Yes, it will smell of old socks, but some rewards are worth the risks.
- And though your school librarian will doubtless disapprove, I would argue to hide a copy or two out of order, tucked somewhere between the history of Mayan civilization and the rudiments of Astrophysics.

Where you hide this book is up to you. Do not doubt that it will be read. It will. The kid that needs this book will find it. They always do.

Thank you, thank you for your extraordinary work with your students, for your ceaseless devotion to Learning. And thank you for allowing us our own small part in the workings of the microcosmic world of your classroom. We will never forget it.

All the best,
The Artists at COMPAS

XIV   COMPAS

I AM A DIAMOND IN THE DIRT

The House

```
        The     The
        roof    roof
       slanted       a
    down             take
     like   The window   off
      a      an    eye    ramp
 mountain    that   looks      for
             through  to        planes
             the     heart
```

The bricks   The bricks   The   The   The
mountainous   hard, and   garden garden garden
volcanoes looking stiff,   full   a   an
over steep   unbreakable of   sign endless
over steep   beau   of   beauty
valleys   tiful end
                             life   less
                                  life

The
sidewalk
a long
path
that will
lead you
where
you want
to go.

Raven Holm, Grade 9
Columbia Heights High School, Columbia Heights
Writer-in-residence: Sarah Fox

If

If I am the sky
    you are the sun that heats the earth
If I am the ocean
    you are the fish that swims in it
If I am the road
    you are the car that drives on it
If I am the orange
    you are the tree I grow on
If I am the trees
    you are the axe that chops me down
If I am the sun
    you are the moon
If I am the clouds
    you are the rain that falls from me
If I am the soil
    you are the flowers in me
If I am a field
    you are the wind that blows gently across it

Craig Arneson, Grade 9
Roseau Secondary School, Roseau
Writer-in-residence: Sarah Fox

Diamond in the Dirt

I am the Diamond in the Dirt that ain't been found
I'm the fight night King that ain't been crowned
I'm that see-through water that's not shallow
I'm that one chunk of food that you can't swallow!

Damien D. Mobley Jr., Grade 7
Central Middle School, Columbia Heights
Writer-in-residence: May Lee-Yang

Untitled

The bad girl came out
of hiding. Woke up, and
gathered fresh roses for
her mother. The sky was
bright blue and shining.

Debbie Le, Grade 8
Metcalf Junior High School, Burnsville
Writer-in-residence: Diego Vázquez

A Long Day

Here is my little brother,
too wild to tame.
He shoves hot dogs
down his mouth, and
they all look the same.
Here is my little brother,
a rocket with unlimited fuel,
but after a good day,
he grabs his
pink blanket,
throws it over his
shoulder like a
backpack and
gets a good
night's sleep.

Leo Guyn, Grade 5
Glen Lake Elementary School, Hopkins
Writer-in-residence: Susan Marie Swanson

My Grandpa's Horses

At night I can hear
my grandpa's horses

running around under
the moonlight sky making
beautiful noises that sound
like a lullaby

Bridger Field, Grade 3
North Intermediate School, Saint Peter
Writer-in-residence: Susan Marie Swanson

Wind

Wind, why are you invisible?
One time you blew my tree
branch off. We had to cut it
and put it in a bag. Why do you
blow bags away and papers away?
Why are you so cold and hot?
You blow a lot and a little.

Alexander Lehman, Grade 1
Aquila Primary Center, Saint Louis Park
Writer-in-residence: Susan Marie Swanson

Stargazer

Lost in the stars
I am not aware where I am going
but I can never keep up
with them.

Madeline Nelson, Grade 4
Meadowbrook Elementary School, Hopkins
Writer-in-residence: Diego Vázquez

Rage

BOOM, my father's
voice is like thunder, my
mother's is like a hurricane
twisting and twirling
into a tangled fire of light.
Crash! The hurricane rages
along a stream, a parade of
madness, then turns to kindle
emeralds, hidden from sight.
Bam! The thunder claps and a flash
of lightning as if trying to burn out.
Any harm that may come to those
close to
him
for
he is
thunder
and she
is lightning.
Together
they storm
on.

Ciera Hardyman, Grade 6
John Adams Middle School, Rochester
Writer-in-residence: Julia Klatt Singer

Fire

I burn to the eyes of the helpless.

I slither like a dragon.

I flow.

I dance like a beautiful princess.

I hover.

I snap like a whip.

I explode with fury and rage.

I shout out like thunder.

I am fire.

Josue Bouteouli, Grade 4
Pilot Knob Elementary School, Eagan
Writer-in-residence: Dana Jensen

So You Wanna Be Bad?

I know this kid named Blake
who had enough time to take
a day off of school
He wanted to stir up some trouble
with his friends on the double
cuz he thought it would make him cool
so he sprayed a full can
and he egged a man
who was a stranger he didn't know
so him and his friends had to clip
for the stranger that they hit
was undercover working for the po-po
They sped through grass
like they were too fast to catch
but when they turned the corner
one of his friends got snatched
so the rest had to dash
cuz they didn't wanna get caught by a grown-up
so they ran to his house
to use as a hideout
until the police came through knockin
his other friend got scared
so Blake left him there
and went out the back as his only option
Now with his friends all caught
and the battle being fought
his only choice was surrender or run
and he knew all along
that when his dad came home
the punishment would be done
But he wanted the attention
of his friends not affection
from any teachers outta his class
so he did what he could
cuz he was so misunderstood
until Mustafa came to pass
he said, "Wo lil homie
you almost ran up on me
so what's the reason for all your panting?"

he told me the story
and how it would all bring him glory
like he was living in a life of action
I said slow your role
you're only 8 years old
and this trouble ain't gonna make you bad
now would you want people to hate you
or rather have them take you
serious as a lil man?
you want the rep and the talk
you gotta walk the walk
and not be a lil hard-headed child
you want the girls and the notice
and everyone to focus
on you for good reasons
so let's remake your style
make people notice you for stopping and
not pursuing
Be a leader, not a follower of what
your friends are doing
you're smarter then this "gotta be bad" act
you got going on
you really wanna be a man? Then accept
what you've done wrong
accept the pain
and realize again
that you're a strong influence on your friends
So take this chance that you're given
and put it in to your livin
and put this knucklehead act to an end
but if you can't do that
and you wanna move back
to your little felony crimes
that you dream of committin
then fine, be what you be
but not a friend to me
and your story will never be written

Mustafa Shabazz, Grade 8
Maplewood Middle School, Maplewood
Writer-in-residence: Lisa Bullard

I Love Nothing

I love the whisper of the dawn
The light sound of the morn
I love the whisper of the dusk
The darkness of the blackened night
I love the sound of just the traveling wind
The whispering of wind between the woods
I love the peace of the forest
Sound only of the breeze and the pine
I love the grace of a flying eagle
Skimming the shimmering clouds of midday
I love silence, whisper, darkness, peace, grace
I love nothing

Jack Lutz, Grade 6
Oak View Middle School, Andover
Writer-in-residence: Dana Jensen

Cake

Emma, the best friend that walked into my life
Since 6, playing with kites
Dress up, Barbie dolls, the things that made us call.
Neighbors in your word, sisters in ours.
We eat mac and cheese from Macaroni Grill,
Computer brings us together, for real and forever.
Remember the hard times?
We had some downers, but we made it up by being clowners.
We love Batman and lightning bolt sprinkles on cupcake.
Piece of cake.

Miranda Lockner, Grade 6
Lake Junior High School, Woodbury
Writer-in-residence: Tou Saik Lee

Master of Science

My brain is a mathematician
struggling with her new equation.
My wishes are a paleontologist
searching in a dry, dusty desert.

My eyes are a microscope
glancing for DNA on the tip of a hair.
My dreams are a computer
on the site of Google.

My thoughts are a rocket ship
just waiting to launch.
My body is the master of science
with all her tools, thoughts and equations.

Emma Olmscheid, Grade 4
Chanhassen Elementary School, Chanhassen
Writer-in-residence: Susan Marie Swanson

The Black Dark Night

In the black
dark night
stars
are
twinkling,

In the sky
I look up
and
a wishing
star
is passing
by.

Tsion Tulu, Grade 3
Valley View Elementary School, Columbia Heights
Writer-in-residence: Diego Vázquez

Garlic

A nice plump mushroom.
A nice big nest in the rainforest
A sack
Spicy air
A mole hole
A huge head with many thoughts
A top
A samurai's head
A paper ball
Crunchy paper
A wheel
An eye

Jasper Zarkower & Ben Ducat-Vo, Grade 1
St. Anthony Park Elementary School, Saint Paul
Writer-in-residence: Sarah Fox

For My Brother

I reminisce about back in the
Days my bro
When we use to kick it
In the playground every day
For sure

Some firm memories
Of back in the days

The moment I heard you
Were gone I broke down
Crying on my knees
Saying Lord please

This can't be reality
I must be living in fantasy
It cannot be that you're
Not really here
It cannot be

Our memories are on my mind
Every day and every night
All of the time you come into my mind

It seems like my voice
Is getting eerie
Every day I think about
That night I get a little
Teary
REST IN PEACE MY BRO
I WILL NEVER FORGET YOU
FOR SURE!!!

*Dedicated to my brother who passed away on August 25, 2007

Edith Hernandez, Grade 7
Central Middle School, Columbia Heights
Writer-in-residence: Tou Saik Lee

Because It Broke

Because I remember the TV saying, "Many missing."
Because I remember the sadness.
Because I remember the videos and the pictures.
Because I remember parts of it in the water.
Because I remember the newsperson saying 20 found
injured, 6 found dead, so far.
Because I remember people giving their cell phones to kids.
Because I remember the school bus on the bridge.
Because I remember family members on TV remembering
their lost ones.
Because I remember the short video clip of it.
Because I remember inspections on other bridges.
Because I remember the 35W bridge.

Samantha Akin, Grade 5
Gatewood Elementary School, Hopkins
Writer-in-residence: John Minczeski

Nana

Nana sits on the couch
Her grandchildren surrounding her.
Her fluffy black and white hair reminds me of
a crumpled newspaper.
She begins the story of her escape from Czechoslovakia.
She looks at the children
who know the story by heart.
They see
the paper dolls,
one of the only things she could bring.
She tells us of the note her father received
forcing them to leave their home for
America.
How they took the *kindertrain*
then a boat.
Of her excitement when she saw
the Statue of Liberty.
And her mother's anger when she threw her brother's hat
in the water for joy.

We hear the *knedlichky* boiling on the stove
The dogs yapping in the backyard.
Her cell phone ringing
but she does not answer it because
she does not know how.

Tessa Ide, Grade 7
Blake Middle School, Hopkins
Writer-in-residence: Susan Marie Swanson

I'm Sorry For The Hairclips

I'm sorry, dear Calvin,
that I made you look like a girl
when you're a boy dog.
I was only five
and I had just gotten new
pink plastic hairclips.
After that, I put a pink floral print dress
on you. Oh, but you looked
like a unicorn in my mind!
And my obsession with them grew!
You couldn't even look at me,
your eyes droopy and embarrassed.
You kept running away when I came back
with new hairclips.
But oh, how beautiful you looked!

Lauren Traiser, Grade 5
Royal Oaks Elementary School, Woodbury
Writer-in-residence: Joyce Sidman

The Mouse

sneaky peekers
trouble makers
white squeakers
peep of the night
the one who eats cheese
running from cats
makes people scream

Mackenzie Murphy, Grade 3
Pilot Knob Elementary School, Eagan
Writer-in-residency: Dana Jensen

First

First to see the waves on the lake
First to see the animals wake
First to see the light of the moon
First to hear the cry of the loon

-Refrain-
Dakota, Chippewa Mohawk too
They were the first ones before me and you

First to feel the wind in the sky
First to see a little one cry
First to see the firelight
First to feel its warmth at night

First to hunt in the early morn
The first people to grow corn
First to chip an arrowhead
First to sleep in a deerskin bed

First ones to ride a horse
First ones to travel a mountain course
The first ones to be well fed
The first ones to be bravely led

Ms. Sweeney's Class, Grade 3
Lincoln Elementary School, Hibbing
Musician-in-residence: Charlie Maguire

You Can't Take a Bully to the Grocery Store

You can't take a bully to the grocery store
The grocery store, the grocery store
You can't take a bully to the grocery store
Because they will smash a watermelon right on the floor

You can't take a bully to Middle School
Middle School, Middle School
You can't take a bully to Middle School
They'll jump and splash the water out of the pool

-Refrain-
You can't take a bully anywhere!
They have mad eyes and an angry stare
They have fists for hands, and kicking feet
You don't even want them on the street

You can't take a bully on the bus
On the bus, on the bus
You can't take a bully on the bus
No one wants them to sit with us!

You can't take a bully to the park
To the park, to the park
You can't take a bully to the park
Because he'll clog the slide, and the dogs will bark!

You can't take a bully to your house
To your house, to your house
You can't take a bully to your house
They won't let you sit down on the couch

You can't take a bully out to lunch
Out to lunch, out to lunch
You can't take a bully out to lunch
They take your tray and eat a bunch

Ms. Welinski's Class, Grade 2
Lindbergh Elementary School, Little Falls
Musician-in-residence: Charlie Maguire

Partners in Crime
(To the tune of "This Land is Your Land")

Chorus
There were two brothers
Two naughty brothers
They were big trouble to their mother
They were so naughty they clogged the potty
They were as naughty as can be

It was really boring in the morning
The boys decided to use some lipstick
To have some real fun with mother's mattress,
They were as naughty as can be.

They took the lipstick and started smearing
Then they decided to start some cheering
Their mother came up to see the ruckus
They were as naughty as can be

Chorus
They went downstairs to the kitchen
Their mother hoped that they soon would listen
But then they poured out a bottle of Noggin
They were as naughty as can be.

They started sliding on their bellies
Their mother came down to make them jelly
She saw the big mess and put them in their rooms
There were as naughty as can be.

Chorus
The boys ran upstairs in a hurry
Their mother started to get worried
Especially when she heard something crashing
They were as naughty as can be.

Molly McFadden, Caity Dorle, Martha Hubbel,
Hannah Lewis, Kelsey Sigvertsen and Annie Kane, Grade 6
 St. Joseph's School, West Saint Paul
Musician-in-residence: Rachel Nelson

That's What Social Studies Is All About

What are the regions of the United States?
If you're walking to California, how long will it take?
In Maine they eat lobster instead of trout
That's what Social Studies is all about!

-refrain-
It's all around, it's all around
It's in the air and down on the ground
Social Studies are all around

You can get there in a truck
Or fly a plane over Las Vegas just for luck
But don't get lost and take the wrong route
That's what Social Studies is all about

Lake Erie has a port
Ontario has a fishing sport
If you swim in Lake Superior, it will make you shout!
That's what Social Studies is all about

"Four Corners" you can touch them all
All down there where the coyotes call
If you go to Arizona, there is no doubt
That's what Social Studies is all about

Valleys, mountains, waterfalls
Fields and islands, you know them all
Plateaus where the geysers spout
That's what Social Studies is all about!

Mr. Nelsen's Class, Grade 4
North Intermediate School, Saint Peter
Musician-in-residence: Charlie Maguire

WHAT THE LONE WOLF DREAMS   29

Lakes & Rivers

-refrain-
Lakes and rivers are beautiful to me
The sunshine that I see
The tall and wide green trees
Lakes and rivers
Morning, noon and night
Eagles and loons in flight
They mean so much to me

The sky in the morning
Is reflected on the lake
A symphony they make
The birds in flight they take
Water splashing gently on the beach
Shells just in our reach
It means so much to me

After morning, the water all is still
Watching from the hill
See the duck's yellow bill
Looking over
To see a beaver build its home
My dog with his bone
A frog recites a poem
It means so much to me

It's nighttime finally
And the day is done
Say "goodbye" to the sun
Bedtime has almost come
Making "s'mores" by the fireplace
Seeing a smiling face
The moon and stars in phase
It means so much to me

Ms. McLeod's Class, Grade 3
Lincoln Elementary School, Hibbing
Musician-in-residence: Charlie Maguire

 **Pretty People**

Todd, he lived in Canada
He is going to take a trip
Down to the "City of Angels"
On that California strip

Courtney is a California girl
Looking for some fun
With her sunglasses and her surf board
Under the California sun
Under the California sun

2.
Todd met Courtney on the beach
She was looking mighty fine
Their eyes met, there was a click
They were together all the time

Soon Todd had to start flyin' back
They said their sad good-byes
He thought about her the whole way back
But she soon met another guy
But she met another guy!

3.
Todd flew back within a month
Looking forward to seeing his girl
But soon he learned the tragic news
A (this) new boy had rocked her world!

Todd he started getting real depressed
(He) thought Courtney didn't care
She just went on ignoring him

Couldn't find her heart anywhere

Couldn't find her heart anywhere!

4.
Courtney and her boy were on a date
When the boy got an idea
He said, "Let's go and rob a bank"
So she said, "Get out of my KIA!"

Courtney left him on the spot
She went to go see Todd
But something just wasn't right with him
Todd was looking kind of odd!
Todd was looking kind of odd!

5.
Courtney said, "I'm sorry Todd.
That boy was a mistake!"
Now we can get back together
And things can still be great
Now they're an "L.A." couple
Looking for some fun
With their sunglasses and their surfboards
Under the California sun
Under the California sun

Lucia Dilorenzo, Aleisha Nelson, Lucy Witchell, Max Brown,
Schyler Sowa, Greg Osborne and Nate Boscardin
Oak Hill Montessori School, Maplewood
Musician-in-residence: Charlie Maguire

Puppies
(To the tune of "Take Me Out to the Ball Game")

Bouncing, growing and shrinking
Running, slobbery barks
Jumping and chasing a ball all day
What could be more fun than playing today?
So let's cheer, cheer, cheer for our puppies
If they bark, it's too bad
There are fifteen
Puppy bowls filled with
Beef chow mein.

The owner out on vacation
There's toys all over the floor
The food bowls are empty
The cat's a mess
The dogs on the floor
Tearing up a pink dress
So let's fight, fight, fight for the slippers
Our owner must come back
There are fifteen
Puppy bowls filled with
Beef chow mein!

Alayna Bjergo, Alanna Dorsey, Rylie Moseng,
Lizzie Nolden and Natalie Stopfer, Grade 4
Northview Elementary School, Eagan
Musician-in-residence: Rachel Nelson

Coon Rapids Dam

Put your boots and snow-pants on
We're going to the Dam, soon we'll be gone
Coon Rapids Dam, by the riverside
Where you can see the deer, but the river otters hide

Walking in a line, with a friend
Trudging through the snow, don't want it to end
Coon Rapids Dam, by the riverside
Where the ducks just float, but the beaver glides

Tasting maple syrup from a tree
It comes from a tap, it's sweet as can be
Coon Rapids Dam, by the riverside
Listen to the Mississippi take a waterfall ride

Remember the good times that we had
Being outdoors makes us glad
Coon Rapids Dam, by the riverside
The "Mighty Mississippi" fills my heart with pride

Mr. Intihar's Class, Grade 3
Riverview Specialty School, Coon Rapids
Musician-in-residence: Charlie Maguire

Penguin

I wish I was a penguin in the ice and snow
Under blue skies, where the ocean goes
If I was one, I'd want you to know
I carry my babies on my toes

If I was a penguin, I'd eat fish
Those finny friends are my favorite dish
And if I had a wish
Flying would be on the top of my list

If I was a penguin
black and white
A penguin
I'd be all right
A penguin
All day and night
A penguin

If I was a penguin I'd start fluffy and gray
I'd swim and sleep all day
And oh by the way
If I could get it I'd eat *"creme brulé"*
If I was a penguin
I'd get nice and fat
I'd waddle around in my "tux" and top hat
I'd stay out late like a cool cat
And when I get home, that would be that!

If I was a penguin
I'd go for a slide
Fat on my tummy, I would ride
Over the ice from side to side
Life is just one big glide
If you were a penguin
You'd like it too
No winter storm would make you blue
If you wanted you could live in a zoo
And I could turn my back to you

Ms. Uncini's Class, Grade 6
Chisholm Elementary School, Chisholm
Musician-in-residence: Charlie Maguire

WHAT THE LONE WOLF DREAMS　　35

Minnesota "Blues"

-Refrain-
We have some news from Minnesota
We'll sing it to you
The Mighty Mississippi, Boundary Waters, Lake Superior too
We'll provide all the information on the Minnesota "Blues"

v.1
Lake Itasca is the source of the Mississippi River stream
It looks just like a cup of coffee, when you put in the cream
I saw this beautiful river, last night in a dream

Direction: "You-You" Girls link arms and turn

v.2
If you like camping and canoeing
This is the place to be
Go to the Boundary Waters, and go paddling with me
We'll go on a portage and we'll live so happily

Direction: "You-You" Girls link arms and turn

v.3
Lake Superior "Gitchegumme"
Is the biggest Great Lake
Sailing on a lake, iron ore you can take
We'll say "Goodbye" now, we hope you stayed AWAKE!

Mr. Johnson's Class, Grade 5
Assumption Catholic School, Hibbing
Musician-in-residence: Charlie Maguire

SINGING TO THE STARS

Making Choices

It was 3:00 and everyone was getting ready to go home. Well, almost everyone. There was a new girl and her name was Jessica. She was nice but she didn't have any friends. Jessica wanted to be friends with the popular kids. They were going to the basketball court to shoot some hoops. Jessica loved basketball, so she followed them.

"Hey, can I play with you?" asked Jessica.

"Sure, but do you know how to play?"

"Yah."

"OK then, let's play!"

A little while later more kids came. It was Jacob and Kyle. They were the bullies. They dared Jessica to skip school the next day. Jessica didn't want to skip school, but Kyle and Jacob dared her to.

"Hey Jessica, don't worry, we'll skip school with you."

"I don't know," said Jessica.

"Come on, you can do it. We could hide behind bushes or go to the skate park."

"I don't skate."

"Oh well."

Jacob whispered to Kyle, "What are we going to do?"

"I know this might be weird, but we could go to the mall."

"The mall?"

"Yah."

"Fine."

"OK, we have $200 you can use at the mall."

The popular girls (Stephanie, Chelsey and Courtney) didn't want Jessica to skip school. "Come on Jess, don't do it."

"Jess?"

"Yah, it can be your nickname."

"Jessica, it's $200—don't you want to keep it?"

"Yah I do, but I just can't skip school."

"I said we would skip school with you."

"I know, but . . . "

"But what?"

"I don't know."

"Come on Jess, don't do it."

"Jessica, it's only one day."

Jessica was getting mad. "You guys, don't put so much pressure on me!"

"Sorry Jess."

"It's OK. I just can't have so many people telling me what to do all at once."

"OK, I think it's time for you to make your decision."

"Right."

"I know it's just for one day so . . . "

"You're going to skip school?"

"OK, see you tomorrow by the mall!"

"No! What am I going to do now? Steff! Steff where did you go? Great, now I'm going to have to skip school!"

The next day Jessica went to the mall, but Kyle and Jacob weren't there. Jessica walked around the mall, but she just couldn't find Kyle and Jacob. Then she decided to sit down for a while. At 3:00 Jessica decided to go home.

Once Jessica got home, she took a nap from her long adventure. In the morning, Jessica was a little scared to go to school.

At school, the principal wanted to see Jessica in his office. Once Jessica got to the principal's office, the principal told Jessica to tell him what happened. Jessica told him everything that happened. Jacob and Kyle got in a lot of trouble, but Jessica only had one day of detention.

Maddie Hartmann, Grade 4
Park Elementary School, LeSueur
Writer-in-residence: Stephen Peters

Don't Get Lost!!

When Jake woke up Saturday morning, he heard, "GET UP, BOY!!" Jake's boss was always harassing him.

Jake quietly said, "Quiet … I will." Jake absolutely hated his boss. He wished it was a family member, even his brother. He wanted to sleep in a warm bed, not a carpet.

"You gonna work or what?" said his boss.

"Yes," said Jake.

"Now you are going to make an iron rod for a customer," said his boss.

"I don't know how. You never taught me," said Jake.

"Well, that's why you came here, right?"

Jake ignored the question and said, "This hammer is too heavy." Dave (his boss) mumbled to himself. All Jake could hear was, "Measly boy …" Dave picked up a lump of iron and steel and hammered them together. Jake heard a deafening pound while sparks flew and hit him.

Jake yelled, "OUCH!!"

"Quiet, you'll wake up the other workers!" said Dave.

"Workers? You never said anything about other workers. Can I meet them?" Jake wasn't sure if he really wanted to meet them, because what if they were worse than Dave?

Dave didn't answer, so Jake just examined the place.

"All right, the rod is done," the boss said in a grumpy voice. "Noo. Boy, come here! My hammer broke and it was the last one. Here is money to get another brown steel hammer for about 8 dollars, first corner, third market."

"All right, boss."

Jake took the 10 dollars and ran as fast as he could. There were no corners, just a straight line. After a bit, Jake forgot where it was, then he came to the first market. "Do I turn here?" he said to himself. "No, it was third corner and first market, I think I'll go with that."

Eventually he reached the third corner. He turned. Jake saw about twenty different markets. "I guess I'll go to the first market."

He opened the door. "Hmm … no hammers … I hope, no, it's probably the next store." Jake was skipping down to the next store and bought a brown hammer.

"Alright! Now I've got it. First corner and third street. Oh no, I've got the wrong place. Now I'll never get home," Jake said quietly, almost whispering. A tear rolled from his cheek.

"I guess I could go the way I got here." Jake was angry at himself. He went over to a few corners. "Ohhhh!!" Jake yawned. Jake looked at the time. It was 9:52 p.m. He was really tired. Jake found a patch of grass as green as slime.

"I guess I could sleep here a bit, just a little nap," Jake said to himself. Jake looked for a pine tree to use for a pillow (because if the points are pointing down it will be soft). He returned to the grass spot and lay down. He slowly fell asleep.

Soon it was morning and Jake's stomach rumbled quite loudly. "Ow, I'm hungry!" Jake complained. "Why do I have this hammer still with me and why am I talking to myself a lot?" After a little bit, Jake wandered back in the woods where he had been sleeping nearby.

Later on that day, Jake ran into a raccoon. Jake had never had any experience with a raccoon before so he didn't know if he should approach it or not. He decided to carefully walk up to it very slowly and as he did, the raccoon scattered backwards very quickly, which startled Jake. The raccoon fiercely hissed at Jake and Jake hurriedly ran away.

Jake continued on his way and looked for any moss on a tree to let him know which way he was headed. "Yes!" screamed Jake. "I found some moss!" He had learned that moss points north, so off he headed. He saw a big white house that he had recognized before. He remembered his home was only a few blocks away, so off he ran. As he approached his house, he collapsed right on his front lawn and was very happy to be home. His mother came out and didn't even know he was lost because he was supposed to be working for Dave.

"Shouldn't you be at work?" His mother said.

Jake replied, "I got lost buying a hammer that had gotten broke."

Mom said, "Let's get you cleaned up and we'll get back to your job. I'm sure Dave must be worried about you."

Jake was so happy his mom was understanding. He had an interesting story to share with his friends as soon as he got off work.

Michael Balder, Grade 5
Hilltop Elementary School, Henderson
Writer-in-residence: Stephen Peters

Molly's New Home

"Ma, why in the world did you buy this house?" Molly whined, thinking to herself that her mom was crazy as Uncle Sam. Uncle Sam was really crazy. I mean, he would put jelly on noodles. No offense if you actually do that.

"Well . . . personally, I thought it would be a nice house to live in. After, well, you know," her mom answered. See, Molly's mom just got divorced with Molly's dad, so Molly's mom doesn't like talking about it.

"I think it's a beautiful house Ma," said Nia, Molly's 13-year-old sister, petting their family's dog.

"Well, I'm happy at least someone likes the house I picked," Ma said, glaring at Molly.

"Show off," Molly muttered.

As they walked into the house, Molly started to complain. "The windows are all smeared. The floors are all creaky. I don't like it here." Molly whined like a three-year-old having a temper tantrum, even though she was twelve. Of course, Ma just ignored her and went on letting the packing guys come into the house. And Nia just did the same being her same show-off self.

The next day was school. In the morning, Molly woke up by the chirping of bluebirds to find piles of boxes and boxes that still needed to be unpacked. Sticking out of one of the boxes sat her poster that she got at a fair. It was a great fair, too. Even if it was as crowded as 150 people in one box. It brought back sad memories of when she and her dad were still in the same house. But she quickly forgot about them and went over to the window to give the birds some bread to eat, and then walked over to her drawer to find some clothes that had been unpacked. She found a horse top with a blue background and some blue jeans that were ripped at the knee. She quickly got dressed and went down the stairs. As she went down, she smelled something really good. It smelled like buttermilk pancakes. She quickly went down and started to serve up some of the pancakes.

"Mind your manners, hon," Ma said, very tiredly. She was still dressed in her pink bathrobe. Nia was so tired she didn't even say anything. "You're going to ride the bus today, hon. I can't drive you to school today because I have an interview with my new boss, Mr. Hemmer." Ma was still trying to wake herself up.

"But Ma," Molly complained like a three-year-old once again.

"No buts, and that's final. Got it? Good. I think I hear the school bus. Get your stuff ready," Ma said quickly this time, being as awake as possible.

Ma was right. The school bus was coming. As Molly was getting on the bus, the bus driver asked Molly where she was from, how old she was, the usual … in a real friendly voice like a teddy bear you'd want to hug right away. She looked old with her white hair, but she wore bright red lipstick and a red polka-dotted dress and not to forget the red jewelry. She was wearing red all over.

Then, all of a sudden Molly had an urge to ask her something. "Is red your favorite color?" Right after then Molly turned bright pink at the cheeks. I mean as pink as a flamingo.

But Mrs. Lemons, the bus driver said, "No, but I do like to be color coordinated. So on every Monday I dress in red. Tomorrow I dress in orange and so on." Molly was really surprised about this, but she didn't care. The bus driver seemed nice enough. Molly tried to find a seat on the bus, but all of them were full so she was just about to tell the bus driver when this boy called her name.

"Hey Molly, over here!"

Molly didn't know exactly who said it, but just to stay on the safe side, she didn't answer. Then the person said it again. "Hey, come over here or you'll be—" he stopped in mid-sentence.

Then a girl said, "Don't mind him. Come sit with me!" Molly listened, not wanting to make any more people disappointed.

She went all the way to the back seat where a girl sat in a big green and yellow sweatshirt saying Packers on the front. She had green pants, too. Molly also was a Packers fan so she decided to start a conversation about them.

"So I see you like the Packers."

"Yeah, I think Brett Favre is the best. Anyways, what's your name? Sounds like you're new here," the girl said.

"I think Favre is the best in the world, too. My name is Molly Henson, although I wish I was named Christy," Molly answered, feeling a strong vibe of proudness.

"Same here. My name is Sally McGuire. I think my last name sucks," Sally said, then adding before Molly could say that she thought McGuire was a way better name than Henson, "Hey, I think we're almost here. What's your schedule? Maybe we're in some of the same classes." Molly thought that was a lot to say in one sitting, but she didn't care. She started to dig through her bag to find her schedule. It looked like this.

Name: Molly Henson

7:30-Auditorium
8:30-Math-Ms. Ramon
9:30-Science-Homeroom
10:30-English-Mr. Gladdy
11:30-History-Homeroom
12:30-Lunch
1:25-Free Period
2:00-Writing
2:30-Buses

It looked exactly like Sally's.

"Oh-my-gosh," Sally said, hypnotized by the sight.

"Well, we'll be seeing a lot of each other," Molly said hypnotized by the sight too.

The day went by pretty normal, at least nothing "unusual" happened, although during lunch a girl named Kenai slipped on a banana and broke her finger. So I guess that could be called unusual. On the way home was normal, too. The girls, Molly and Sally, didn't end up doing anything unusual except working on their five pages of History homework. It was pretty easy—if you were an adult, that is.

When the bus stopped at Molly's house, the girls both smelled an aroma of freshness. To them the bus was all hot and stuffy. As they were stepping off the last step of the bus, Molly asked, "Do you want to come to my house for dinner? I could show you my Mom and my—um—a sister?" Molly forgot she didn't live in Charleston any more with her dad.

"Sure, that would be great. I have a sister, too. She's a year younger than me, though. She can be a pain in the neck," Sally said grimacing. "But I get through it."

"Same here. My sister is a year older than me. She always thinks she's Miss Perfect. I wish I was an only child sometimes," Molly said in a sad voice. The girls started to go towards Molly's house, then Nia stepped out.

"Why are you here so early?" Molly asked in a sassy voice.

"In a matter of fact, I get out of school at 2:00, so I get home early," Nia said back in an equally sassy voice, adding, "Who's this anyway?"

"This is Sally McGuire. She's a friend from school," Molly said glaring at her sister.

Then the two girls went into Molly's room. "You know, I think I'm going to like it here," Molly said, really meaning it.

"You'll learn to love it here," Sally said.

The two girls worked on their homework and then they had spaghetti for dinner. And that was the way it was for those two. Going over to each other's house every other night, for the rest of the year.

Grace Kirkpatrick, Grade 5
Meadowbrook Elementary School, Hopkins
Writer-in-residence: Stephen Peters

Singing to the Stars

It was 1960 and I was twelve years old. I lived with my mom in a small apartment building in New York. It was about ten o'clock at night and I couldn't sleep because of the noises in the room next to us. We had just moved here, so I decided to get up and explore. I scooted out of bed and walked to the small window. I sat on the floor, and felt an iron plate under the rug. I moved it and saw a small iron door, no bigger than our wash bin. I lifted the latch and slowly opened it. It went really far down. I couldn't see how far, but I tried to be brave and reach in. I gasped as I touched something that was metal and cold. I grabbed hold and pulled out a long mass of piping. It looked like a musical instrument that I had once seen in a dance show … it was a trombone!

Holding it awkwardly, I wiped off the dust and cobwebs and tried to remember how the men on the TV held it. I put the mouth-piece to my lips and blew. *Berrggh!* The noise scared me so much I almost dropped it.

From that day forward, I played every day, but we could never afford lessons. Even though I sounded terrible, Mama always liked it.

One day, Mr. Magorsy knocked on our door. He was the land-lord, you see. He wanted to talk to my mama. Mama told me that I couldn't play the trombone in the building because the neighbors were complaining.

"But Mama, where else am I supposed to play?"

"You can go to the back alley and practice. But don't go past the laundry mat!"

"Yes, Mama."

After chores, I went out behind our building and started to play the song I made up called "Boogie Swing Ding." Walking while playing, I went past the laundry mat. And I kept going when I heard different music besides mine. It sounded really good. I started to dance and play my trombone with it.

I followed the music to a club called Rhythm and Blues. I hesitated to go in. But I had to find out who played that music. I walked slowly in and the music got louder. I saw a bunch of tables and in front of them all, a stage with a man hitting drums, another playing a huge violin, a man with a saxophone, and one man dressed in light blue playing a trombone. I walked forward but a big man stopped me.

"Are you with the jazz band?"

"Ah … um …"

"Well, get up there. They started without you!" He pushed me forward and lifted me on the stage. I couldn't move. I stood there and noticed that the song sounded a bit like "Boogie Swing Ding," so I played along. I imagined I was on the moon playing for the stars, looking down on the earth. Then the music stopped and I heard clapping. I got pushed off to backstage. I was in a small room that smelled like smoke. All the men who were on the stage were around me.

"Say, little brother, where did you come from?"

The man with the sax took my trombone and examined it.

"I'm from the apartment down the alley with my mama."

"What's your name, son?"

"Jonas, sir,"

"Well," the man with the trombone said, "where'd you learn to play like that?"

"I just found it and practiced a lot."

"Well, how'd you like to play with us?"

"I'd have to ask my mama first, but I'd love to!"

A week later, I was in lessons. I hated them—all those lines and dots and curly cues.

"Now play this and that," Miss Finster would say. When I played my own music, she'd get mad and would go over and over the lesson all day.

My first concert! I went with the Blues Brothers to a different club and we played on stage. We played "Bill Bailey's Bones" and I was dancing with the clouds and singing to the birds. It was a Monday night, and I was fifteen years old then, with legs as long as broomsticks.

I was coming home late and Mama was lying on the floor, with the sink still running. I called the police right away, and an ambulance came. They brought her to the hospital.

I never left my mama's side. The doctors told me she had a heart attack but should be all right.

"I love you, Mama," is what I told her a million times. One night I woke up to a loud beeping and a lot of noise. A bunch of nurses ran in and out. *Mama! Mama! What's wrong?*

The next day, Mama was dead. They said she must have hit her head when she fell. I played at her funeral, but I didn't stay for the whole thing. I went home and put my trombone back where I found it.

I didn't leave the house for a week, and missed two concerts. Eventually, the trombone player from the Blues Brothers came to my house.

"I'm sorry, son, but it wasn't your fault. It's no reason to stop your playing."

"I should have been here. I could have caught her or got the ambulance sooner."

"No, son, you can't give up your music. Music is what keeps you groovin', and don't you remember that your mama loved it too?"

So now, thirty years later, I still live in this same apartment. I still have legs the length of broomsticks. My trombone is never out of my hands, and I know my mama is on the moon, singing to the stars, looking down on me on the earth.

Mollie Rae Miller, Grade 8
Roseau Secondary School, Roseau
Writer-in-residence: Kelly Barnhill

Kelsey

Me? I was in love with her, of course. That much was obvious. But girls like that don't go for guys like me. Or at least I was pretty sure they didn't. Well, it started the way most stories begin, on a bright, sunny day that seemed like nothing could go wrong. My best friend, Nick, was playing with me on the basketball court at our school. Boy, were his shoes dirty, not to mention stinky.

Well, this girl named Kelsey ran over to us. Yes, she is my "friend." Anyway, she came up to us and said, "You'd better get inside. Mr. Murphy will take attendance soon." Mr. Murphy is my fifth grade teacher. Don't tell him, but I think he's kind of strict.

We all ran inside just when Mr. Murphy was looking for me. Mr. Murphy is very tall. He stood towering over us. "Late again?" he asked. He wrote on a piece of paper and gave it to me. It said, *Matt, Nick and Kelsey are late again. Please take care of the situation, Mr. Rogers. Signed, Mr. Murphy.*

Oh, no! Mr. Rogers is the school principal! This is bad—really bad! We all shivered as we walked down the hall. When we got to the principal's office, I took a deep breath and opened the door. I handed him the note. We had a little talk. Suddenly, Kelsey said, "It was all my idea."

My jaw dropped. Kelsey is one of those kids who is good all the time. We walked into the hall. Nick ran all the way back to our classroom without a word. Before I left, I said thanks. Then I quickly ran down the hall.

I knew the next day was Valentine's Day. What should I get her? A book? A hat? Earrings? When I got home, I took a walk by the brook to think of ideas when I saw something glittering in the stream. It was a stone! It's perfect! She'll love it!

I ran home as fast as my legs would run. I found a pencil, cardstock, foam hearts and a pair of scissors. I was working so hard that I didn't see my sister sneaking up behind me. She took my card and said, "Are you making a love note?" I snatched it away from her.

"Get away," I said through gritted teeth.

"Fine. I'm going to tell the whole world that my brother likes a girl."

The next morning I woke to the sound of my sister singing. Today was you-know-what day. I quickly brushed my teeth, grabbed a granola bar and headed out the door. I heard my sister say, "Boy, will he be mad when he finds out." At school, I looked in my backpack for the card. Oh no! Where was it?! Just then, Kesley came up to me and handed me a box. I was curious of course, so I opened it. It was a bunch of cookies! I said, "Thank you," and ran off.

Well, that's the story.

You want to know what happened to the stone? My sister took it out of my backpack and made it into a necklace. She told everyone she got it from her boyfriend. Now I can tell the whole world that my sister likes a boy!

McKenna Ryan, Grade 4
Chanhassen Elementary School, Chanhassen
Writer-in-residence: Kelly Barnhill

Relationship

My friend Cassidy and I are crazy together! Recently when I was at her house we had some pretty interesting moments, but I'm getting ahead of myself. Let me start from the beginning.

Enchanted was finally out, and me and my friend Cassidy were both eager to see it. So I was talking to her on the computer one day and we had decided to see a movie at 2:50. We were crossing our fingers for the monster screen, and when we arrived and got tickets and started heading to the theatre we realized we got the huge screen. We were thrilled, but turns out that we were a little later than everyone else. It was packed in there so it was hard to find seats for three (Cassidy, me, and her sister Carolyn).

"I see some," hollered Carolyn, and we were all excited to see this movie. Once we got to our seats the film started. *Just in time*, I thought. It started and we giggled and even cried (or at least I did), and we both decided that it was a wonderful flick. Once we left the theater we waited to get picked up. Her parents were already there and my dad was nowhere to be found so she yelled, "I have an idea! You could just come and sleep over at our house," and that is exactly what we did. I went over to her house and then the fun started …

We felt a little nutty so we made Christmas lists even though it was November still; then we exchanged them so we could buy each other gifts. I ran into Cassidy's room and put on an old hot pink tank top dress with a green flower smack dap in the middle. It had a matching pink jacket of the same color that, too, had a green flower on it. She put on a bluish greenish skirt with a matching jacket. The bathroom was wide open so I jumped in and packed on make-up. We put on bright blue eye shadow, hot pink blush, red lipstick and black mascara. "We look like such dorks," we said at the same time.

Since it was Thanksgiving the other day, she still had plates, teacups and a teapot out, so we had a tea party! Carolyn cut the cake into small pieces so we could all have four. OK, so none of us like tea, so we had the really good juice in this old blue teapot. Her parents thought we were really weird, but knowing us it was expected. Next, we had a fashion show! We tried to look silly and that's sure right. I think we looked horrible. That's the fun part of it all. We did that for about an hour, and then got bored. So we drew on their gigantic white board, there was nothing really that we were drawing, just some really goofy things like rainbows and butterflies.

Secondly, it was time to set up the beds. "Let's sleep under the table," I suggested. That's basically what we did. We brought a little TV so we could watch a movie, and we covered the table with blankets so it would be dark. That was super fun and I will never forget how many times their dog Missy came in and knocked over the blankets so we had to re-do it about ten times. At about 2:00 we thought it was time to go to bed, so we watched a movie called *Material Girls*, then squeezed under the table for the night.

In the morning we got up and ate some donuts and went outside to play on their swing set. It was freezing cold, but it was still fun taking pictures with their new camera. I have great friends and I am thankful for each one. These are some of the weird things we like to do and I will never forget this day.

Joey Strand, Grade 7
Eagle Ridge Junior High School, Burnsville
Writer-in-residence: Louis Porter II

The Birth of My Brother

I was four and all I can remember is being shoved into my grandpa's car. Before that I was told that I was going to have a little brother. *What's a brother?* I thought in my mind. I tried to picture what a brother looked like. First I thought of a stuffed animal, but didn't think there was an animal called brother. Then I pictured another person. *Would my family really want another person? They already had me,* I thought.

My grandpa's car normally smells like coffee and cigarettes. But that day it smelled clean and fresh. Why did my grandpa clean his car? And why was his hair nice and fancy? Why is his mustache gone? Was this all for the brother?

We arrived at a hospital and it looked like a horror house. We parked far back in the parking lot. Inside a nurse directed us where to go. We took an elevator and arrived in a hallway with lots of doors. I didn't pay attention to the numbers on the doors, so I don't know which room we entered. My mom was holding a small person with five little brown hairs growing on his head. My dad said that I could hold him as long as I was careful. So I took him in my arms. He stirred, opened one eye and looked up at me. I knew why my family wanted him and I knew that I wanted him in my family.

Justin Jochim, Grade 6
Glen Lake Elementary School, Hopkins
Writer-in-residence: Laurie Lindeen

Positive Thoughts

"Ouch!" I yelped as I fell to the ground on the skateboard ramp.

"You're so funny!" said Jesse Arons and his gang. That's probably why they always invite me here—to come and laugh at me.

"I have to finish some math problems for my homework," I said.

"You actually do your homework?" Jesse said in a funny way as I was walking home.

I'm so relieved to be home! Someday I'm just going to say that I'm coming and I won't show up. But then they'll beat me up at school. I just don't know what to do. I wish I had a friend to talk about this, but everyone thinks I'm too nerdy for his or her kind of style. I know! I'll act cool during school so the big kids will actually respect me.

"Bob? Is that you?" a shrill voice said from the living room. That's not Mom, it's Grandma! She came all the way from California. She just fled the forest fires and is coming to live with us. She has given us a lot of money to help pay for the apartment since Dad died. He died of cancer. I could smell the chocolate chip cookies baking. They were like smelling a cup of hot chocolate after you have been freezing out in the cold for a week. Grandma always makes them when she comes to visit because she knows I love them.

My mom said to me later that evening that our house was on the line of a fishing pole. One day I might wake up in the middle of a field. Even all that money from Grandma didn't help. She said that one day she'd buy a mansion in Minnesota and let us come and live with her. I'm just hoping that that will actually happen. My grandma is 89 years old. She probably doesn't have much of her life left. That's why we have to cherish her visits.

The next day at school, my teacher says that I have to go home immediately and I have to come back for my stuff. I end up running home through the icy, cold weather. It was like Dracula blowing on my neck and giving me goose bumps. When I get into the apartment room, I see Grandma laying on the floor, my mom on the phone with the paramedics. I see an ambulance pull up from the street. They are now knocking on the door. When they leave with Grandma, my mom rushes me into the car. It smelled of leather so strong that I thought my mom was cooking liver in there. On the way to the hospital, I ask my mom what happened.

She said that Grandma was in the kitchen baking cookies, and that she was folding laundry in the living room. All of a sudden, THUMP! She heard something crash to the floor. She ran into the kitchen about as fast as Flash on Batman and Grandma was lying on the floor.

"I thought she was dead!" she exclaimed. "Then I called the paramedics and called your teacher. I'm scared, Bob," she said in a worried kind of way. "I don't think she is going to make it." Then a nurse came rushing out.

"Your mother is dead. We think she hit her head when she fell. It caused her brain to shut down. I'm sorry." Could my life get any worse? I can't skateboard, I'm nerdy, have no friends, and now my grandma just died! I'm not even going to try to be cool anymore.

You know what? Why go through life if it's not worth living? I'll try not to act so weird, but still be an A student. If I'm ever going through hard times, I'll just remember that Grandma and Dad are always watching over me. I have to think about the good times when they made a good choice and how I can follow that idea. All I have to do is believe in myself. If this ever happens to you, always remember to believe in yourself and to set goals.

My goal is to ignore Jesse Arons and maybe to practice my skateboarding!

Nicci Falk, Grade 5
Liberty Ridge Elementary School, Woodbury
Writer-in-residence: Stephen Peters

My Story

The bright LED display on my alarm clock read 12:26 AM. I turned the knob on my window lightly, trying not to make too much noise. An ambulance sounded in the distance.

"Hurry up, Patricia!" whispered my best friend, Alex, from the ground. She was clad in the usual—ripped jeans and a lacrosse sweatshirt.

"I'm coming," I hissed back. As I went to lower myself out of my second storey window, my foot slipped.

"Whoa ... Look o—" I lost my balance, falling from the windowsill onto the grass, taking Alex with me.

"Ow!" she complained. "Coordinated much?" She stood up and brushed herself off, as I sat there, trying to keep my fingers from trembling.

"I don't think we should do this," I admitted. She sighed.

"Tricia, you told me this morning you would come with me." I could make out her glare in the darkness. "Come on. Please? For me?" Alex had been my best friend forever, and I didn't want to let her down.

"Oh, OK," I said, giving in. She smiled.

"Good," she said. "But if you change your mind again, I'm throwing you in the river."

I laughed.

"Come on." We made our way down the street, her carrying a backpack with her. It bounced up and down on her back as she walked.

"Change your mind yet?" she asked as we neared the river. I thought about it for a second.

"No, I think I'm good," I replied.

We finally approached our junior high. We both paused, taking a deep breath.

"You ready?" she asked, taking two cans of blue spray paint out of her backpack. I took a deep breath.

"Yeah, I guess," I answered. I held out my hand for the spray paint can. The cold metal felt like ice on my hand.

"So, you never told me what you were planning on writing," I pointed out. Ignoring me, she walked up to the outer wall of the school, her finger poised on the can.

A stream of indigo liquid sprayed from the end of the can when I looked closer. I saw that she had the letter "S." Following that was a "T." Then an "O." She shook the can. Following the "O" was a "P," a "T," "H," "E," "W"…

My alarm clock sounded like fingernails on a chalkboard the next morning. I groaned, reaching one lazy arm over to turn it off.

Maybe just a few more minutes, I thought to myself, and rested my head on my pillow.

"Patricia! Patricia!" shouted a familiar voice from the hallway. I sighed.

"What?" I replied lazily, eyes still shut.

"Come down, now! Look what happened to your school!"

Walking into the living room, I heard the smooth voice of the reporter.

"Students in that age group are becoming more and more opinionated," he was saying. A picture of my school popped up. "STOP THE WAR" was written all over it in blue spray paint.

"There are different ways to make a point," my mom was saying. She picked up her laundry basket and headed out of the room.

"School today will be cancelled due to clean-up necessities," the anchor informed. I turned and darted out of the living room, upstairs to my bedroom.

I hit speed dial #3 on my cell phone. A few moments later, Alex picked up.

"Hello?" came a tired, hoarse voice from the other end.

"Alex! Alex!" I whispered. "We're on the news! Well, we're not. The school is! It's cancelled today because they need to clean it! Alex, what if we get caught? What if we get expelled?" I exhaled. Alex hadn't made a noise. "Alex?" I asked.

"Tricia, I don't care," came the reply.

"What? What do you mean you don't care?"

"I just don't care," she repeated. "I've lost everything. My dad …" She trailed off. I knew why now.

"Oh, Alex, that's right. I forgot," I said.

"Whatever." And with that she hung up.

Shaena Swanson, Grade 8
Central Middle School, Columbia Heights
Writer-in-residence: Lisa Bullard

The Surgery

My eyes were transfixed on a white screen that revealed the hidden truth showing through the transparent film. It was time for the doctor to deliver the news. Bad news.

"Caden, I think you're grown up enough to hear the truth. After all, you know better than all of us how you really feel," said Dr. Sanjay. He didn't pause for my reply, or maybe he did and I couldn't speak because I was frozen in my place, in fear of what he might say next.

"Caden, your spine is crushing your lungs. You will die if we don't operate soon." He delivered the sentence swiftly, cutting through the confusion of my mind with painful clarity.

The curtains surrounding the exam room hung heavy with misery. I felt like I might suffocate from the silence in the room. Somehow I found the courage to speak,

"So, basically, what you're saying is that I'm twisted and there's no turning back. No second chances."

My mother's sobs interrupted my speech. She sat next to me holding her head in her hands, crying like a wounded animal. My father was looking up at the doctor. I could see that his jaw was tight with tension. I felt his thick hand resting on my shoulder, trying to steady me from the shock that was my reality.

I looked down at the floor and thought to myself, "This can't be happening. I wore my brace every day like the doctor told me to." Tears rolled down my cheeks and I fell forward in my wheelchair with weary resignation.

On surgery day, I sat in my wheelchair nervously poking at my IV. I was in Pre Op. A nurse wearing pants and a top covered in cats approached. A freaky feline hung from her stethoscope, and she slid him close to my face to check my heart. I grimaced as the cold metal touched my chest.

"Nice strong heartbeat, Gary," she said.

"Well thank you. My name is Caden," I said stiffly.

She frowned. "According to our records…"

I cut her off curtly, "I go by Caden, not Gary."

"Caden honey, it's OK," my mom interrupted. "The nurse doesn't know about your given name and what we call you."

"All right, we'll call you Caden," said the nurse.

"I am Caden," I retorted.

"OK, whatever," she continued, "according to your medical history you're seven years old and you have Spinal Muscular Atrophy, Type II. Today you're having a spinal rodding. Any allergies? Are you taking any medication?" She droned on like a robot on automatic pilot.

My father scooped me up and gently laid me on a gurney. A guy in a green mask approached. "Ready for take off?"

"I guess so," I said, sounding like a reticent passenger.

We pulled into a room full of doctors and nurses. Bright lights glared from above. I felt like a helpless animal facing a pack of predators.

Then I heard Pastor Rich's soothing voice. "Hey buddy, this is the day God made for you!"

"Pastor Rich, I'm scared," I whispered nervously.

"But you're ready, aren't you?" he said with enthusiasm. "Remember all of our good talks over the past few weeks; remember your hopes and dreams for the future?"

I looked into his face for guidance and found strong reassurance. "Yes," I said,"I do have a strong faith that God is with me." Then I paused and looked at the surgical team. "But Pastor Rich, is God with them?"

"We're ready!" said a team of gowns and gloves.

"Caden," Pastor Rich asked, "do you want to pray?"

"More than anything, but I want my team to join us."

Everyone stopped. This incredible circle of people closed around me like a warm rainbow of colors. Faces from around the globe looked at me, and Pastor Rich let out the words. The room was an ocean of emotion and I felt faith rise up within me and in everyone around me.

Caden Sager, Grade 6
Glen Lake Elementary School, Hopkins
Writer-in-residence: Laurie Lindeen

Fox

The fox stole the speed of a cheetah
and left it limp.
He drank in the color of the setting sun
and used it for his glistening red coat.
He gathered the shadows from the deepest
part of the forest
and used it for his slyness.
He swallowed the darkness of the night sky
and used it for his eyes.
He took the jagged peaks of the Rockies
and carved them into his claws.
He carved his teeth out of solid stone
and left the stone as nothing but sand.

Lucas Reiners, Grade 8
Nicollet Junior High School, Burnsville
Writer-in-residence: Dana Jensen

Meeting my Other Piece

I met my other piece
on the sidewalk one day.
It was like filling in a hole
that had been dug awhile back.
I don't know how it got there
all I know is this,
it's not there anymore.
It is all filled in and nice,
with a new piece of grass on top.
The day I met my other piece.

Madison Smith, Grade 8
Metcalf Junior High School, Burnsville
Writer-in-residence: Diego Vázquez

The Time Chaser

I am the only time chaser.
I ride a tiger.
I only go at dawn.
I'm skinny as dust.
I have a black cape.
I love to see you sleep
but I'm gentle, not known to bite.
I may fly but only when I need to.
I'll make the light disappear.
I may have long nails, but only to scare you.
I may be old when I see you.
I'll love to see you again
but for now, goodbye, my good friend.

There it went and disappeared
into the dark night sky.

Bordeaux Crouse, Grade 4
Liberty Ridge Elementary School, Woodbury
Writer-in-residence: Joyce Sidman

If I Was

If I was a black bear
I'd crawl on trees and eat
blueberries. I'd go to camp
sites and sit staring
at the sky, tossing around
food that I found in the
cooler.

If I was a turtle
I would creep
on the soft sand in the Bahamas.
I would step one toe in
the water to make sure
it was warm. I would
go deeper into the water
watching magnificent fish
swim by.

If I was a cheetah
I would run faster and
better than any other cheetah.
I would pounce on my
prey like a little girl
pouncing on a pony
at a petting zoo.

If I was an owl
I would be able to stay
up all night watching with
my laser eyes, peering
at everything in my path.

If I was a snake
I would slither in the steaming
desert sand at sunset
in Arizona.

Julia Laden, Grade 5
Tanglen Elementary School, Hopkins
Writer-in-residence: John Minczeski

Dream Poem

In the night sky
We flew in a plane
It went off course
And sped through the air

I realized I was the only one
As it spun and flipped through clouds
I yelled for help extremely loud
But there was no one around

I was only yards away from the ground now
I knew it was the end
Now I was feet from the ground
I closed my eyes and prepared for the worst
I opened my eyes and I was in my bed
With a loud beeping
My alarm had woken me up

Ben Bergeland, Grade 7
Eagle Ridge Junior High School, Savage
Writer-in-residence: Louis Porter II

The Three Magical Foxes

Once upon a time there lived three foxes. Their names were Lillian, Lily and Lola. Lola was the youngest, Lily was middle age and Lillian was the oldest. They were not just foxes, but magical foxes, and they loved having adventures.

One day Lily tried to sneak outside, but Lily was not the only one trying to get out. Their mom locked them in their room. They could not use their magic. Lillian tried spells, but the spells did not work. It was Lily's turn. Lily tried to throw glass at the wall, but it did not work.

Then it was Lola's turn. She said, "Why don't we just ask if we can go outside?"

"No, no, no. Mom will never let us out," said Lily.

"I know, let's just fly up to the window," said Lillian.

"How will we get out?" asked Lola.

"We'll just break the window," said Lillian.

"This better work," said Lily. They beat their wings, they got high and higher until they got there. Lillian and her sister used their magic. The windows did not lock.

"Finally!" said Lily. Then they flew to their friend's house. Their friend's name was Jared. They got there and asked where the Great Owl lived. He said the Great Owl lived in the Golden Palace.

"Well, that's not too far," said Lily.

"Wait! He will get mad if visitors come," said Jared.

"What will he do?" Lillian asked.

"You'll see," said Jared.

"Well, what are you waiting for, let's go!" said Lily.

"OK, OK," said Lillian. "Goodbye!"

Then they flew out. It took them three days to get there. Finally, they got there.

"Well, we're here," said Lilly.

"Sssshhhhh!! We might get in trouble!" said Lillian.

Lola just looked around wondering if she could play with anything. "Well, we haven't gone any farther. Lola and I will go home," said Lily.

"OK," said Lillian. She kept going and soon her sisters were gone.

Later she came across the Steel Woods. Everything in the Steel

Woods was made out of steel. Anything or anybody who tried to pass by would be attacked. Lillian didn't want to fly, it was too high and there were steel birds. Lillian felt uncomfortable near the Steel Woods. She took a deep breath and took off running. Squirrels threw acorns at Lillian, but they didn't hurt her. Birds pinched her head and she tried running faster.

Then she came upon a fox. Every move she did, the other fox would do. It was harder to get past the other fox. Then she remembered that she had magic. She said a spell that went like this: *Spell speaks to me soon, if not split this fox in two!* All of a sudden, the steel fox split in two! It was never seen again.

Lillian worried if she would have to fight any other vicious animals. "I'm glad that's over," Lillian said. She flew away and landed near a pond, and she waited for the next bad thing to happen. She waited and she waited, but nothing happened. She thought it was safe to start going. Lillian looked around and felt lost. "I wish I was with my sisters," said Lillian.

Meanwhile Lily and Lola had to practice magic for leaving the room. They wished they had stayed home. Their mom asked where Lillian was, but Lily and Lola didn't know.

Lillian kept going. She was tired. Then a huge shadow appeared. She looked up and there she saw some woods. They weren't just any woods, but the Mean Woods. She ran as fast as she could, but two birds dropped an ice cube so that Lillian could slip and fall. She was about to hit a tree, but she jumped before she hit it. She used a spell again. She said a silly spell: *Spell listen to my wish, make these birds get fish!* Then the two birds flew away. Lillian ran out of the woods before the others.

Shisana Urrutia, Grade 2
Franklin Elementary School, Anoka
Artist-in-residence: Jerry Blue

Wind

I wish I were the wind
Free and running all the time
Playing on the treetops
Running on glassy waters
Stirring them into chaos
Warming coastlines, freezing plains
Sometimes stopping to get a rest
But quickly back up to
Run again

Javan Baker, Grade 7
Roseau Secondary School, Roseau
Writer-in-residence: Dana Jensen

I Was Reading a Poem

I was reading a poem
about a flower
and a lily opened up—
it was bright red.

I was reading a poem
about monkeys and a monkey
swung on a lamp in my house.

I was reading a poem
about dolphins and the dolphin
splashed me in the face.

I was reading a poem
about feathers and feathers
fell out of the sky on me.

I was reading a poem
about a butterfly and a butterfly
flew right past me
as fast as an airplane.

Erika Kuske, Grade 2
Pilot Knob Elementary School, Eagan
Writer-in-residence: Dana Jensen

My Backpack in the Evening

My backpack at
night is resting in
the chair's lap.

It's thinking about
all the things it
carried home.
My shoes, my snow pants,
my yellow folder,
and all my other mail.

Its shadow looks
like a big whale
shooting up water
from its spout.

Lily Den Hartog, Grade 2
Glen Lake Elementary School, Hopkins
Writer-in-residence: Susan Marie Swanson

Ode to the Cowgirl Boots

They sit in a bin
on a shelf
in a closet
like a forgotten
treasure,
as clean and white
as my mother's pearl necklace.
Vivid memories
of a little blonde girl
with a smiling face
being sent off to kindergarten
live
inside those boots.

The boots have been
homes
for tiny feet to dwell inside.

Now they lay as still
as the ground beneath the snow
in winter.

Krista Rud, Grade 7
Blake Middle School, Hopkins
Writer-in-residence: Susan Marie Swanson

Today I Am a Slug

I feel so slow today.
I'm as slow as the world going around the sun.
I'm so tired. I could go to bed on my desk.
I would like to go home already.
I go slower than a toddler.
I go slower than a baby.
I go slower than a mushroom growing,
or a flower, or a tree.
Today I am a slug.

Grant Rosenberger, Grade 2
St. Joseph's School, West Saint Paul
Writer-in-residence: Joyce Sidman

Avalanche Adventure

"Bye, Mom! I'm going to snowboard with Josh!"

"But Brad, you haven't finished your home …" That was all Brad heard because by the time his mom was done talking, he had already grabbed his snowboard and was heading off to his friend's house.

As he was running, he felt someone stick their foot out and trip him. "Oof! Ow! Ah! Oh!" Brad called out as he rolled over various rocks and bumps. He got up and rubbed his sore arm. On top of the hill he saw his two older twin brothers laughing like lunatics.

"I'll get you some day!" Brad shouted up at them, shaking his fist.

"Hi Brad, what's up?" his friend Josh said, walking around the corner.

"Nothing much, just my two brothers playing tricks on me. Want to get to it then?" Brad asked.

"Yeah, I found a new way down the mountain through a small forest," Josh replied.

While they were walking, they saw various signs saying DAN-GER! AVALANCHE AREA! but Brad and Josh were keen to try out the new route, so they ignored the signs.

"Here it is," Josh announced, pointing down a steep slope.

"Wow, dude, this is huge!" Brad exclaimed.

"The bigger the better," Josh said as he took off down the slope.

As soon as Brad looked back, he regretted overlooking the avalanche signs.

"Josh! Avalanche!" Brad shouted. Josh looked back and his face turned pale.

"Almost there," Brad muttered, even though he knew they wouldn't make it.

He looked back, and wasn't surprised that the front of the avalanche was only twenty feet away.

As they entered the forest, Brad knew there was no escape. He heard the roar of the snow directly behind him. All of a sudden, he fell. As the avalanche passed over him, it felt like a five-ton weight slamming down his back. He rolled around under the snow for a bit, and then blacked out.

"Brad … Brad … Can you hear me …?" came the muffled voice of Josh. Brad opened his eyes and saw that he was trapped in a pocket of snow.

"Brad!" came the voice again.

"Over here," Brad mumbled back.

All of a sudden, Josh's face popped up.

"How did …?" Brad began.

"While you were snoozing, I was digging a hole trying to find you. Anyways, you are closer to the top so let's start …" Josh was interrupted by a loud thump. Snow fell from the top of the air pocket.

"Hey! Help! We're trapped!"

After what felt like a long time, the top of the snow broke and Brad and Josh could see something other than snow. What they saw was the worried faces of Brad's two older brothers.

"Guys," said Brad, "for once I am really happy to see you two."

Tony Cauthorn, Grade 4
Grey Cloud Elementary School, Cottage Grove
Writer-in-residence: Stephen Peters

Jovan Finds a Friend

Once there was a worm named Jovan. He moved to a new school. Jovan had no friends. When he was walking into his new school, he came across an ant.

"Will you be my friend?" asked Jovan.

"No way!" said the ant. "I would never be a friend with a worm!"

Jovan was very sad. I'll never find a friend, he thought. When he got to the classroom, he came across a spider.

"Will you be my friend?" asked Jovan.

"Never!" said the spider. So Jovan was really sad now.

When it was recess time: "Hey! Slimmy boy!" said a big ant.

"Try the monkey bars!" said a spider. "I know you can't do it."

Jovan did the monkey bars. They were amazed! They never thought a worm could do that. "Wow!" they said. Jovan was amazed too.

After that, Jovan went to the swings. He sat down and swung up and down. He was swinging so high and so fast he lost his grip and slipped off the swing and flew into the air. His head landed in the cold sand. He realized that he could make tunnels in the sand. He tasted damp sand all recess, digging tunnels. He loved it!

Suddenly Jovan heard a voice yelling, "Help!"

"I wonder who is yelling for help?" said Jovan, so he followed the sound. He finally reached the sound and it was a big, poison-ous spider that was wrapping another worm in silk! I have to save that worm, thought Jovan, so he slid across the underground tun-nel. Suddenly a big rock flew at him. He ducked and curved his tail. The rock turned around and came flying at the spider. The spi-der was hit by the rock. When the spider was unconscious, Jovan untied the worm from the silk. They both escaped from the spider and they went back to the playground. They saw the spider crawl-ing through the tunnel, so they covered the hole with dirt.

"Thank you for saving me," said the worm.

"You're welcome," said Jovan, and from that time forward the two worms were friends.

Grace Sinclair, Grade 2
Madison Elementary School, Blaine
Writer-in-Residence: Stephen Peters

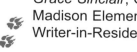

The Spooky House

The rain was pouring down like their mom turning the hose on full blast. There was mom Rasky, dad Rasky, brother Wyatt Rasky and Anna Rasky. Mom had received a great job offer. Anna was all for it until *boom*, she hit them with the moving part of the story.

"This is it kids, 5432 Cherokee Road."

"What," Anna yelled, "we have to live in this four floor, creepy, one thousand year old house!"

"Honey, you were being positive about it just an hour ago," said Dad.

"Well, you didn't have to move away from your school, your favorite hang-out, even worse, your BFFL (best friend for life)."

"Well now you can make new friends, or even better, pick a room with Wyatt out of fifty-two."

So Wyatt and Anna dragged their feet up the stairs like they weighed more than an elephant at the zoo. *Creek ... creep ... crick ... crock* went the stairs. The two siblings looked in every room until Anna found the room she liked.

It had a walk-in closet, an area great for her desk, a little lounge area for her bed, and the rest of the space for playing. Anna was so excited; she spit out a double kick flip spin from her gymnastic routine. The room went dark when Anna tripped on something she didn't recall seeing before. *Crick* went her leg.

"Ow, my leg. Wyatt, help I can't get up," screamed Anna as high as an opera singer throbbing with pain.

"Don't be afraid, we are your friends," said a high-pitched spooky voice.

"Who are you and what do you want?" Wyatt came rushing down the hall as if flying through the air he was running so fast.

"What is wrong and what is that horrible smell?" asked Wyatt, searching for Anna in the dark.

"What is going on here?" asked their worried parents.

"I was so excited about my new room that I did a trick from my new routine and then right when I was about to land I tripped on something that wasn't there before so I screamed as loud as I could until someone started talking to me and then a horrible smell came and ..."

"That's alright honey, we don't need to hear the whole story," her mom said, interrupting Anna.

"Let's get you downstairs and I'll call the doctor," said her worried father. But just as they were helping Anna out of the room the voices came back.

"Where are you going, don't you want to stay with us?"

"What's going on?" asked her mother.

"It's the voices again."

"You mean you were telling the truth?" asked Wyatt nervously.

"Of course I was. I wouldn't lie about that."

The room suddenly was filled with this horrible fragrance like sour milk. The family was alarmed that such a thing could happen. Even with Anna's injured leg, she and her family ran like the wind down the stairs into the front yard. All of a sudden the house started twisting and turning as if they made the ghost mad.

"There is some story behind this house and I'm going to find it after I get something to put on my leg for now."

Anna and her family went to their local bandage store and bought a wrap for her leg.

"Now, where are we going to find out information on this house?" said Wyatt, trying to be detective Svecksa, which is from a movie.

"Well I, for one, think we should go to the library," said Dad.

"That's a great idea. Let's go," said Mom. The family got in their car and drove to the library.

Once they walked into the library, a strange man with a dusty old navy blue suit on walked up and said, "Hi, I don't know who you are, but I have this strange feeling that you need help getting information on the house of 5432 Cherokee Road."

"Yes, how did you know that?" asked confused Anna.

"Well, I didn't want to tell whoever was living there this, but I used to live there.

"The first night I was there someone started to talk to me. I was too afraid to do anything so I just ran out of the house to a family member's. And now every time I go past that house, I can feel this strange feeling like someone looking at me. As a matter of fact, the last time I drove by a high-pitched spooky voice started talking to me telling me that a family was going to come here and they needed help searching for information on the house."

"That must have been the voice we heard. I wonder why the voice told you we needed information on the house?" Anna said, confused.

"Maybe the voice needs help about something it can't get done by itself," said Wyatt.

Anna almost jumped from the thought.

"Well, now that we are investigators, we need investigator

names," said Dad.

"OK, my name is Roxy Hunter," said Anna.

"Then my name is Detector Svecksa," said Wyatt.

"And Mom and Dad are just Mom and Dad," said the two siblings.

With fright in their stomachs, the family went back to the house, back upstairs, back into Anna's room. Once they got into the room the voices came again. "Welcome back."

Wyatt the Detector Svecksa spoke up. "Who are you and do you need help?"

"My name is Penny. I need help finding my family crest."

"Do you know where we can find it?"

"Yes. There is a man at the library. He always wears a dusty old blue navy suit."

"The man at the library," yelled Anna. The Rasky family once again ran in their car to the library.

"Ah, I had a feeling you would come back. Here is the family crest."

"Why did you keep it all this time?"

"Because I can't give it to my sister Penny. Someone else has to give it to her. This is the task Penny has to do to be accepted in haunting another house. Once you give it to Penny, I will go away forever. Now hurry back before it's too late!"

"Come on, let's go," yelled Anna, hoping it's not too late.

Anna and her family ran into the car and drove back to the house. Wyatt jumped out of the car and ran as fast as he could go up the stairs to the house. The whole family huddled together when that high-pitched spooky voice came back.

"Here is your family crest, Penny," said Anna.

"Thank you, now my brother can be free from this world. You have earned your ways of this house. Now I will go away if you want me to."

The family talked about it for a minute and came to a decision. Anna spoke up, "Actually Penny, we would like you to stay. But no playing any spooky tricks on us."

Then Penny spoke up, happy to be able to stay. "You'll never know!"

Brenna Colleen Viola Falk, Grade 4
Gatewood Elementary School, Hopkins
Writer-in-residence: Stephen Peters

Snake

Snake began.
He drank the glimmering water of the ocean
to make his swiftness along the wilderness
grasses.
He inhaled the wind of a dark Fall night
to make his horrifying hiss.
He stole two black holes from the depths of the universe
to make his wretched eyes.
He gathered volcanic rock from
the deepest volcano
to make his slick fangs.
He took shingles from a house
and placed them along his skin.
He grabbed a hundred cold souls
and made his blood.
And the snake was made.

Chasson Brown, Grade 8
Nicollet Junior High School, Burnsville
Writer-in-residence: Dana Jensen

The Stolen Sapphire

In the place where magic was rumored to exist, a girl named Jaime lived. The small village was called Salmia. Her family was richer than most people in their community, and she was always pampered, known as the pretty girl with auburn curls, but she didn't want that. She wanted to be known for a good thing, for she was a generous and clever person. She never acted spoiled and the neighbors were always intrigued by it. She also had a younger sister, Anna, whom she loved dearly.

One night while Jaime and her family were dining, there was a soft tap-tap-tap at the back door. This was very unusual, for visitors always came to the front door.

Mama said, "Jaime, could you go see to whoever that is?"

She replied, "Yes, Mama."

She went into the hall and headed towards the back door. She unlocked it and looked out. The visitor was dressed in a tattered black cloak and spoke with a raspy voice. "Miss, can your family spare a space for the night and let me rest here?" He was clearly a man.

"No, we can't. I'm sorry. Have a good night," she said. Before she shut the door, she looked into his face to see what he looked like. Her blood went cold. She glimpsed a flash of red and felt a creepy, weird chill in her bones. She quickly shut the door and went back to the dining room were she found Mama, Papa and Anna looking at her expectantly. She didn't tell her parents or sister much except that a strange man had come to the door, asking for a place to spend the night.

Later that night, she went to the writing room where her parents wrote letters, had meetings, and so on. She headed to the safe room to check on the magical sapphire her family guarded. She had had a strange feeling about it ever since the mysterious visitor. When she opened the lock, *the sapphire wasn't there!* The cushion lay empty. Jaime went back to her room after locking the safe again.

She thought about what to do about the sapphire. She knew it could do a lot of harm if in the wrong hands. *I have to do something about it. Get it back*, she said to herself. "How?" was the question. Her mother had given her a present a week ago for her fifteenth birthday, saying, "Open it when you feel you need it. It's an object that has been passed on for generations to those who are of adventurous spirit. Use it well." She now opened her trunk and took the package out. She ripped it open. She knew what it was at once. It was a disguiser and a tracker. Jaime had read about it in one of her mother's books of magical objects. She knew what to do before her mind quite got the grasp of it. She held it and said, "Invisibility." Her body disappeared. She left her room swiftly and went to the back door. It opened silently to her touch. She was going to hunt down the mysterious man and get the sapphire back.

"Track the footsteps," she whispered. The potholder, which was the disguiser and tracker, led her on. She went on, thinking what a powerful object she had. Her home was heavily guarded at night and she had gotten out easily. The potholder, on track mode, led her to the inn in the village square. A man was walking to the inn, too. She waited until he opened the door and followed in silently behind him. The tracker told her to go upstairs. It led her to room 13. She paused and listened; she heard snoring. She quietly said "Open," and the door opened. Jaime stepped inside.

The room was lit with only one candle. The potholder took her to his bedside cabinet; the man was sleeping soundly. She instinctively knew that the velvet pouch on the cabinet held the sapphire, a feeling of power emanated from it. She took a peek and she saw a glint of blue; she was right. She was so excited she hurried quickly to the door just as the man bounded off the bed. He knew Jaime was there.

She ran as fast as she could, out the inn door, through the village square, and back to her house. She shouted, "Open!" and burst into the hall, slamming the door behind her. She came face-to-face with the mysterious man.

Jaime froze, utterly shocked. His hood was completely off and she was looking into the face of her uncle, James Malloy. She asked quietly, "Hello, Uncle James. Why were you dressed like that?"

"Hello, Jaime," he replied. "Your parents wanted me to take a look at the sapphire and study its qualities. They asked me to come by. I used magic to remove it from its safe when you opened the door. I'm dressed like this because I'm a detective working undercover for a magical research institution."

"Oh," Jaime replied lamely.

"Does that answer your question?" Uncle James asked.

"Uh-huh," she said.

The next morning, Jaime's mom came in to talk to her; Uncle James had spent the night there. She sat on Jaime's bed.

"Did you figure out it was a set-up yet?" her mother asked.

"Yes, Mama. Why, though?" asked Jaime.

"Salmia is known for its myths and legends. You just made a legend yourself. It is now written in the Salmia records. A mysterious man waits for a beautiful daughter of the Malloy family to turn fifteen. Then he ambushes her, and she is never seen again. You've made legend."

Jaime smiled. She fully understood now. She felt truly blessed to be part of the Malloy family. "Hmm, I wonder what you have in store for Anna," Jaime said.

Mama just smiled mysteriously.

Jenny Nguyen, Grade 5/6
Highland Park Elementary School, Saint Paul
Writer-in-residence: Vanessa Ramos

My Teacher the Alien

One breezy May morning, Lilly walked into school. As she approached the classroom, she felt something wasn't right.

"Ms. Fallbrooke?" Lilly asked, but her favorite teacher wasn't in sight. Suddenly everyone ran to their desks. Lilly slithered like a cobra searching for prey. The door creaked, and a tall, dark-haired woman walked in.

"Sit down everyone," said the strange woman. "My name is Miss Grey, and Miss Grey only," she hissed to the class. Lilly's best friend, Susan, raised her hand.

"What happened to Ms. Fallbrooke?" quivered Susan.

"That is a private matter," Miss Grey said quickly.

Later that day, Lilly saw Miss Grey run suspiciously into the bathroom. As she followed slowly, she heard a loud screeching noise. It sounded like the *American Idol* contestants who don't make it to Hollywood. As Lilly approached the stall, she saw what looked like skin dropping from the top. Lilly looked through a hole in the stall, and what she saw was frightening. As the screeching continued, Lilly ran out of the bathroom. Miss Grey's face was yellow and purple, and the screeching was her talking!

Miss Grey is an alien! Lilly quivered as she thought about the problem to herself. *And what happened to Ms. Fallbrooke could have brought her to Mars!* thought Lilly.

When Lilly was walking to lunch, she heard a strange rattling in the janitor's closet. As she opened the door, she was afraid of what she would see because the last time was way too scary to even think of! *Creeakk!* The door was rusty and needed some oil. The closet was dark, except for a beam of light coming down from the ceiling, and Ms. Fallbrooke was inside of it!!!

"Ms. Fallbrooke?" Lilly questioned.

"Yes Lilly?" Ms. Fallbrooke said coolly. "Flip the switch on the wall to get me out of this force field!" she said with relief.

Lilly hit the switch, and she and Ms. Fallbrooke ran out of the small closet. Just then, Miss Grey walked by, and Lilly pulled the alien teacher's face off in front of everyone. Miss Grey, the alien, ran outside and never came back!

Cameron Frost, Grade 4
Bailey Elementary School, Woodbury
Writer-in-residence: Stephen Peters

One Day

One day we went swimming.
My mom said that I swim
like a great gray dolphin.
I had not noticed that I did.

Then mom told us to get in the car,
time to go home. When we were in the car,
the sun was sitting in my lap
while my mom was driving the car.

That was my big secret
because nobody noticed
that I had the sun in my lap,
but I did.

Hli Chang, Grade 3
Highland Park Elementary School, Saint Paul
Writer-in-residence: Julia Klatt Singer

Forest

Forest,
how are you so
lush and green
through all of you,
through your trees?
Why are your wildflowers
so colorful for us to enjoy?
And why are your
bears so scary?
Please don't let people
cut down your
trees, harm your nature,
spray your bees,
and pick your flowers.
I remember seeing
your beautiful deer.
Your clouds are
a wedding veil.
Your scarlet leaves
are blush.
Your soft green
grass is your dress.
I love to go outside
and smell your pines.
My grandma tells me stories
about a girl named
Shoolee who lives in you.
She always knows her path.
Shoolee rides on beautiful does
through the forest,
and on dark, dark nights
when the moon is full
you can almost hear her
praising the forest.

Rachael Anderson, Grade 4

Oak Hill Community School, Saint Cloud
Writer-in-residence: Susan Marie Swanson

The Magical Tree

Once there was a monkey named Jake. He lost his favorite hat. He cried and cried. "Oh, no! Where is it? I looked everywhere . . ."

Suddenly, his mom called and said, "Jake, time for dinner!"

"OK, Mom!" said Jake.

Then Jake ate dinner and said to his mom, "Mom, I lost my favorite hat and I can't find it anywhere!"

"Oh, it's OK. Don't worry, we'll find it in the morning."

Then Jake went to bed. That night a little boy came into Jake's backyard and took his hat.

The next morning Jake woke up and went out to his backyard. He said, "I remember where it is!"

Jake looked behind his favorite tree, but it wasn't there. Then he heard a voice that said, "Go back to your favorite tree and climb into it."

So Jake climbed back up the tree and the tree started to fly. It flew all the way to St. Louis. Jake felt very scared!

But a friendly boy came walking along. "What's your name?"

"My name is Jake."

"My name is Mark."

"Have you seen someone walk by with a hat that has MN on it?"

"Why?" said Mark.

"Because a voice in my head said, 'come to St. Louis.' So here I am. Hey, that little boy has my hat!"

"Let's go!" said Mark. So they ran after the little boy.

Suddenly, the little boy stopped and said, "OK, I'll give you your hat back."

"Thanks!" said Jake.

Then Jake ran back up his favorite tree again and flew back home. He was very happy. Jake never lost his favorite hat again.

Katelyn Tarrolly, Grade 2
Oak Hill Community School, Saint Cloud
Writer-in-residence: Stephen Peters

The Announcement

Anastasia couldn't stand it anymore! She got up and left the table. As she walked down the rather long corridor, she thought to herself, *Why does SHE have to be so mean?* Anastasia was a girl—not just an ordinary girl. She was a grand duchess living in 1918 in Russia. Her sisters were Annabelle, Corrina and Tianna. Anastasia absolutely loathed Corrina! Annabelle was her favorite sister. That was probably because they were both the same age, thirteen. Corrina was the oldest at seventeen and Tianna was the middle child at fifteen. Her father was the Tsar of Russia.

Her mom had left when Anastasia was three. Her father had just remarried to a woman named Alexandria. Anastasia was in her room glaring out the window when there was a knock on the door.

"Anastasia, it's Annabelle. May I come in?" That was exactly why Annabelle was Anastasia's favorite sister.

"Why must she be like that? Is it because she's the oldest?" Anastasia practically yelled. The reason Anastasia got mad was because Corrina didn't like what the cooks were serving, so she complained throughout the whole meal and didn't eat a thing. Annabelle tried to calm Anastasia down.

"We both know that Corrina's never ever nice to anyone and she never will be, so all we can do is stay out of her way."

Tianna came into the room. "Father wants us at once. He says he has an important announcement." Annabelle gave Anastasia a sideways glance. Their cat came prancing down the hall. They could tell she was coming because of the bell around her neck. Anastasia snatched her up and prepared for the announcement.

Anastasia, Tianna, Corrina, Annabelle and Snowball came down the stairs and went directly to the meeting room. When they got there, Alexandria and their father were waiting for them.

"As you may know, WE have an announcement," Father said. "Alexandria is pregnant." He motioned to his new wife. Snowball got up and left the room as the girls stood in shock. This wasn't what they expected.

The next day, they were all packing to go on vacation for a celebration. Anastasia and Annabelle weren't too happy about this whole thing, but they pretended to be. When they heard a loud knocking on the door, the girls jumped. "Annabelle, Anastasia, are you girls ready?" Tianna asked.

"No," they chimed together. They were going to Poland. They always wanted to go there, but not with Alexandria.

Later on the next day, they arrived in Poland. It was one of the many houses that they owned that they stayed in. There was a little river by the house. *Great*, thought Anastasia, *That's all I need —to stay with Alexandria!*

Today was the day for sailing! Annabelle and Anastasia were playing down by the river. There were little rocks sticking out of the water that they could jump from here to there.

"I bet that you couldn't jump as far as I could," Annabelle challenged.

"Oh, yes I could," Anastasia shot back. Right after she said that, Annabelle jumped one rock ahead of her. They carried on like this for about five minutes until it all came down to one rock in the middle of the river.

"If you make that rock, I will give you my pearls."

Anastasia looked at the rather slanted rock, then at the deep dark river. She jumped and hoped for the best.

Perfect landing! Or so she thought. Anastasia landed on the rock perfectly, but since it was so slanted, she slipped right off of it and fell face first into the water. The currents were too much for her. She got swept down stream and the water was freezing!

"Anastasia!" She heard Annabelle cry as soon as she got around the bend. She struggled to stay above the water. Gulping for air, her heart sunk as soon as she saw what was ahead.

A huge rock the size of a tree split the river in two. Before the rock was a small log. She reached for it, but missed. The rock was coming at her. She was about seven inches away from it when strong arms picked her up. It was one of the guards of the palace on a small boat. "Try to be more careful next time, Anastasia," he said with a worried look in his eye.

"I'll try," she responded, shivering.

One week later, Anastasia had pneumonia from the cold river. The servants stayed in the room with her most of the time, and Annabelle did, too. Alexandria came in once or twice. She was one month pregnant

There was terrible news the next day.

"Alexandria was outside with Annabelle today, picking flowers, when all of a sudden Alexandria fainted! Annabelle didn't see it but she heard a thud and the guards came running." Tianna sat on Anastasia's bed, telling her the story.

"Is the baby alright?"

"I—I—I don't know!"

Anastasia felt awful! All that time she was hoping for the worst, and the worst finally happened.

The next day, Anastasia felt much better and wanted to go and visit Alexandria. No one came to tell her anything that morning, so she decided to find out for herself. She walked and walked and walked, until finally she arrived at the door.

How pale she is! Anastasia thought. Alexandria took a turn for the worse. "Alexandria?" Anastasia whispered.

"Yes?" Alexandria faintly answered. Alexandria looked so frail that Anastasia didn't know what to do.

"Are you alright?" Anastasia asked.

"I'm hanging on," she whispered. Anastasia made an excuse to leave. She couldn't stand to see her suffer.

The priest was praying over Alexandria that night.

"The doctors came in and gave her two more hours of life," Annabelle wept.

"Two hours!" Anastasia gasped. "She was fine this afternoon." Anastasia burst into tears. She loathed Alexandria at first, but now she felt so sad! Their father came into the room. "You girls have five minutes of visiting time to say goodbye to Alexandria," he said.

Anastasia shakily went into the room and wept beside her. Sadness overcame her. She had nothing to say but, "I love you, mother."

The royal family stood there one year later at the anniversary of Alexandria's death. They stood over two gravestones: Alexandria and her son, Jeremiah.

Alicia Dorr, Grade 7
Central Middle School, Columbia Heights
Writer-in-residence: Kelly Barnhill

The Day Cambree's Artwork Came to Life

This is Cambree. She is a famous artist who lives and breathes art. She draws, paints, sculpts and does artwork of all sorts. Cambree lives in sunny California and has artwork displayed all around the world. She has created beautiful masterpieces of all sorts. Cambree was known for how realistic her art looked.

But everything changed on the morning of Friday the 13th. All of Cambree's masterpieces had come to life!

Her "Kangaroo From Down Under" drawing in Australia hopped out of its picture. Her "Panda From The Bamboo Grove" mosaic in China crawled out and ate some bamboo. Her "Alligator From The Everglades" sketch in Florida crept out of the water. Her "George Washington" portrait in Washington, DC, stepped out of his frame. Her "Hannah Montana" sculpture in Nashville, Tennessee, came out and sang. Her "Nona Lisa" painting in Paris, France, awoke from her deep stare. And the scariest of all, Cambree's own self-portrait in her bedroom had come to life!

It was 9:00 AM and Cambree had just woken up. She got up, brushed her teeth, got dressed, and went to go eat breakfast. Little did she know she wasn't the only one up. When Cambree went to put her dish in the sink, she heard a noise come in the other room. The TV was on and someone was on the couch watching it!

"Are you kidding me? That is the WORST self-portrait I've ever seen! The face is all wrong, the hair is a mess, and it doesn't even look like you!" exclaimed the mysterious person.

Cambree stood frozen in shock at the fact that someone was in her house watching and criticizing her TV.

"If I, Cambree the Spectacular, was painting your portrait, it would look so lifelike you wouldn't know if you were really you or if the painting was you!" the unknown person shouted.

Cambree couldn't believe her eyes. "What on Earth are you doing in my house and who are you?"

Then the mysterious person jumped up and turned around to see Cambree angrily standing behind her.

"Hello, I'm Cambree, I just thought I'd come watch some TV while I was up. You know I've been dead still in that frame in your room for years. I got pretty bored of it," said the now-known person.

"How … How … How did you get out? You're not even real. You're only a painting," Cambree said, stunned.

"I'm not only a painting, I'm you," replied the painting of Cambree. "I'm your self-portrait."

"How did you get out?" questioned Cambree.

"It's Friday the 13th, duh!" the portrait said.

"I know what day it is," Cambree stated.

"Don't you know," continued the painting, "on Friday the 13th of June, we come alive?"

"But how? Why?" asked Cambree. "Do all paintings come to life?"

"I don't know. It just happens because it's Friday the 13th of June. And no, only your paintings become alive. The others have their own day," answered Cambree's portrait.

"How do you know?" wondered Cambree.

"We talk," replied the portrait.

"Wait, so my other pieces of art are alive, too?" worried Cambree.

"Yep, all of them," informed the painting.

"Oh no!" shouted Cambree. "They can't be alive, people will see them! How do we make them back to normal?"

"Brownies!" the portrait said.

"Brownies?" questioned Cambree. "If I give them brownies, they will turn back to artwork?"

"They sure will," replied the painting. "If you gave me one, I would too. But it has to be before the end of the day or they will stay alive till the next Friday the 13th in June!"

So Cambree and her self-portrait hurried into the kitchen and cooked up some brownies. In no time they had whipped up a few pans of brownies. By now it was noon and they had to hurry and get the brownies to the art!

First they took a ferry to Australia to give her "Kangaroo From Down Under" a brownie. But first they had to find it.

"There are hundreds of kangaroos," complained Cambree. "How am I supposed to know which one it is?"

"What did you name it?" asked the painting.

"I named it 'Kangaroo From Down Under'," replied Cambree.

"So ..." said the portrait, "call its name."

"KANGAROO FROM DOWN UNDER, WHERE ARE YOU?" Cambree yelled.

Then a normal looking kangaroo, no different than the others, hopped up to Cambree and her self-portrait.

"Are you 'Kangaroo From Down Under'?" questioned

Cambree's self-portrait.

The kangaroo nodded its head and Cambree quickly grabbed out a brownie and handed it to the kangaroo that then gobbled it down. POOF! And the kangaroo was gone.

"Did it go back to the museum?" asked Cambree.

"Yep, it should have," answered the painting.

Then they headed for China in a plane. Once they got there, they headed for the bamboo grove.

"PANDA FROM THE BAMBOO GROVE!" screamed Cambree. A large panda crawled over to Cambree. She handed a brownie to it and POOF!

Next they took a boat over to Florida. They paddled into the Everglades and started to search for the alligator.

"ALLIGATOR FROM THE EVERGLADES!" shouted Cambree.

Just as she did, a large alligator swam up to the side of the boat. Cambree quickly tossed a brownie into its mouth. POOF! It was gone.

Next they hopped on a tourist bus to Washington, DC. Since they were looking for George Washington, they decided to look for him at the Washington Monument. In the distance they saw a tall man wearing a navy button-up shirt and a white wig.

"That must be him over there!" exclaimed Cambree.

"Are you George Washington?" questioned Cambree's portrait.

"Yes, I sure am," replied George.

Cambree scrambled to get out a brownie and handed it to George.

"Brownies are my favorite!" George said as he POOFED back to the museum.

Next, they rode horseback over to Nashville, Tennessee. Hannah Montana wasn't hard to find because she was standing right outside the museum, surrounded by a large crowd.

"HANNAH!" yelled Cambree. Hannah hurried over to see what they wanted.

"Here," said the painting, "have a brownie."

Cambree grabbed a brownie and hesitated as she gave it to Hannah. "First, can I have your autograph?" asked Cambree.

So Hannah gave Cambree her autograph and Cambree gave Hannah a brownie.

"I love brownies!" shouted Hannah as she POOFED away!

Cambree and her self-portrait went to hop on a plane to Paris, France. Once they got there, they headed to the Eiffel Tower. After searching around for a while they found Nona Lisa.

"Nona, is that you?" asked the painting.

"Yes, I am Nona Lisa," she replied.

"We have a brownie for you," Cambree said.

"Yum!" replied Nona Lisa.

Cambree quickly handed a brownie to Nona Lisa. She gobbled it down and POOFED back to normal.

Finally they headed back to California to Cambree's house.

"Well, now that we got that all taken care of, what are we going to do?" asked Cambree.

"I don't know. Don't I get a brownie?" replied the portrait.

"If you want," replied Cambree, "but then you'll turn back into a picture."

"That's where I belong," said the painting, "and I really love brownies."

"Me, too," agreed Cambree.

So Cambree and her self-portrait sat down at the kitchen table with a glass of milk and a brownie. POOF! And that was the last of Cambree's self-portrait. Well, at least until the next Friday the 13th in June.

Jenny Anderson, Grade 8
Skyview Middle School, Oakdale
Writer-in-residency: Lisa Bullard

Spell for the Heart

Be a butterfly flying through
the air on a nice spring day.
Be a cat purring like
a song. Be a backpack
holding all my love
in it. Be a clock telling me
when it's my time.
Be a joy in the world.
Be my life. Be my heart.

Megan Sowada, Grade 4
Holdingford Elementary School, Holdingford
Writer-in-residence: John Minczeski

What the Lone Wolf Dreams

The lone wolf dreams of cold
crisp nights where the full moon
glitters on the snow.

The lone wolf dreams of cool
waters untouched by human hands.

The lone wolf dreams of autumn
leaves twirling above his head.

The lone wolf dreams of running
across the barren land but never
feeling sleep.

The lone wolf dreams of howling
at the moon and getting a reply.
The lone wolf dreams of being
part of the pack, part of the whole.

Jolie Richter, Grade 7
LeSueur-Henderson Middle School, LeSueur
Writer-in-residence: Dana Jensen

Index by Author

McLeod's Class, Ms.	Lincoln Elementary School 30
Miller, Mollie Rae	Roseau Secondary School 46
Mobley Jr., Damien D.	Central Middle School 4
Murphy, Mackenzie	Pilot Knob Elementary School 23
Nelsen's Class, Mr.	North Intermediate School 29
Nelson, Madeline	Meadowbrook Elementary School 9
Nguyen, Jenny	Highland Park Elementary School 81
Olmscheid, Emma	Chanhassen Elementary School 16
Reiners, Lucas	Nicollet Junior High School 62
Richter, Jolie	LeSueur-Henderson Middle School 96
Rosenberger, Grant	St. Joseph's School 73
Rud, Krista	Blake Middle School 72
Ryan, McKenna	Chanhassen Elementary School 49
Sager, Caden	Glen Lake Elementary School 58
Salzman's Class, Mrs.	St. Joseph's School 28
Shabazz, Mustafa	Maplewood Middle School 12
Sinclair, Grace	Madison Elementary School 76
Smith, Madison	Metcalf Junior High School 63
Sowada, Megan	Holdingford Elementary School 95
Strand, Joey	Eagle Ridge Junior High School 51
Swanson, Shaena	Central Middle School 56
Sweeney's Class, Ms.	Lincoln Elementary School 26
Tarrolly, Katelyn	Oak Hill Community School 87
Traiser, Lauren	Royal Oaks Elementary School 22
Tulu, Tsion	Valley View Elementary School 17
Uncini's Class, Ms.	Chisholm Elementary School 35
Urrutia,.Shisana	Franklin Elementary School 67
Welinski's Class, Ms.	Lindbergh Elementary School 27
Zarkower, Jasper	St. Anthony Park Elementary School 18

Index by School

Metcalf Junior High School	Debbie Le 5
Metcalf Junior High School	Madison Smith 63
Nicollet Junior High School	Chasson Brown 80
Nicollet Junior High School	Lucas Reiners 62
North Intermediate School	Bridger Field 7
North Intermediate School	Mr. Nelsen's Class 29
Northview Elementary School	Mrs. Hembre & Mrs. Scheuring's Classes 33
Oak Hill Community School	Rachael Anderson 86
Oak Hill Community School	Katelyn Tarrolly 87
Oak Hill Montessori School	Mr. Albright's Class 31
Oak View Middle School	Jack Lutz 14
Park Elementary School	Maddie Hartmann 38
Pilot Knob Elementary School	Josue Boutouli 11
Pilot Knob Elementary School	Erika Kuske 70
Pilot Knob Elementary School	Mackenzie Murphy 23
Riverview Specialty School	Mr. Intihar's Class 34
Roseau Secondary School	Craig Arneson 3
Roseau Secondary School	Javan Baker 69
Roseau Secondary School	Mollie Rae Miller 46
Royal Oaks Elementary School	Lauren Traiser 22
Skyview Middle School	Jenny Anderson 91
St. Anthony Park Elementary School	Ben Ducat-Vo 18
St. Anthony Park Elementary School	Jasper Zarkower 18
St. Joseph's School	Grant Rosenberger 73
St. Joseph's School	Mrs. Salzman's Class 28
Tanglen Elementary School	Julia Laden 65
Valley View Elementary School	Tsion Tulu 17

Program Writers 2007-2008

Kelly Barnhill
Jerry Blue
Lisa Bullard
Sarah Fox
Dana Jensen
Tou Saik Lee
May Lee-Yang
Laurie Lindeen
Charlie Maguire
John Minczeski
Rachel Nelson
Stephen Peters
Louis Porter II
Vanessa Ramos
Joyce Sidman
Julia Klatt Singer
Susan Marie Swanson
Diego Vázquez

The Lillian Wright Awards for Creative Writing

These awards are intended to recognize the finest literary achievements among young writers in Minnesota. The Wright Awards are underwritten by the Lillian Wright and C. Emil Berglund Foundation. Award winners from *What the Lone Wolf Dreams* will be formally honored at the December 2008 Publication Celebration.

COMPAS is proud to honor the winners of the fifteenth annual Lillian Wright Awards for Creative Writing, given to the best examples of student writing featured in the 2007-08 COMPAS Writers & Artists in the Schools anthology, *What the Lone Wolf Dreams*. The 2007-08 winners are:

Best Prose in Grades 1-4: "The Spooky House," by Brenna Colleen Viola Falk, Grade 4, Gatewood Elementary School, Hopkins

Best Prose in Grades 5-6: "The Stolen Sapphire," by Jenny Nguyen, Grade 5/6, Highland Park Elementary School, Saint Paul

Best Prose in Grades 7-9: "Singing to the Stars," by Mollie Rae Miller, Grade 8, Roseau Secondary School, Roseau

Best Song: "Penguin," by Ms. Uncini's Class, Grade 6, Chisholm Elementary School, Chisholm

Best Poetry in Grades 1-3: "Today I Am a Slug," by Grant Rosenberger, Grade 2, St. Joseph's School, West Saint Paul

Best Poetry in Grades 4-5: "If I Was," by Julia Larson, Grade 5, Tanglen Elementary School, Hopkins

Best Poetry in Grades 6-7: "Nana," by Tessa Ide, Grade 7, Blake Middle School, Hopkins

Best Poetry in Grades 8-9: "So You Wanna Be Bad?" by Mustafa Shabazz, Grade 8, Maplewood Middle School, Maplewood

Awards Judge: David Bengtson, longtime Creative Writing teacher and COMPAS contact person at Long Prairie-Grey Eagle High School, as well as a former member of the COMPAS Board of Directors and the author of a book of prose poems, *Broken Lines* (Juniper Press).

WAITS Anthology Order Form
Tear out or copy this form and return it with your payment

Name:_____

School/Organization:_____

Address:_____

Phone number/E-mail: _____

Quantity	Year	Title	Price
_____	2008	What the Lone Wolf Dreams	12.00
_____	2007	Eyes Full of Sky	12.00
_____	2006	The Wind Tells Me Stories	12.00
_____	2005	My Mind Can See in the Night	12.00
_____	2004	Sing to the Dust	12.00
_____	2003	In My Hand Forever	12.00
_____	2002	Good Morning Tulip	10.00
_____	2001	Northern Lights	10.00
_____	2000	Give Me Your Hand	9.00
_____	1999	I Stand on You and Sing That Song	9.00
_____	1998	River Pigs	9.00
_____	1997	A Special Stretch of Sky	9.00
_____	1996	Rooftop Jailbirds	8.00
_____	1995	Oh, Light Sleeper, Wild Dreamer	8.00
_____	1994	The Dream of the Whale	8.00

Earlier issues are also available, please call for information!

_____ Class Set (min. 10 copies of each book) at 25% discount

_____ Total cost of books ordered
_____ Minnesota Sales Tax (7%)
_____ Postage and handling *($2 first book, $1 each additional)*
_____ **I would like to make a tax deductible donation to COMPAS!**
_____ **TOTAL DUE**

Please make checks payable to COMPAS
Mail orders to: COMPAS, 75 West 5th Street, #304, St. Paul, MN 55102

Your support allows us to continue offering affordable programs to schools throughout Minnesota! Thank you.